THE LAST
TEMPTATION
OF RICK PITINO

ALSO BY MICHAEL SOKOLOVE

PENGUIN PRESS | NEW YORK | 2018

THE LAST TEMPTATION OF RICK PITINO

A STORY OF CORRUPTION,

SCANDAL, AND THE BIG BUSINESS

OF COLLEGE BASKETBALL

MICHAEL SOKOLOVE

PENGUIN PRESS
An imprint of Penguin Random House LLC
375 Hudson Street
New York, New York 10014
penguinrandomhouse.com

Photo credits
Insert page 1 top: © 2018, Scott McIntyre for *The Washington Post*, Reprinted with Permission;
1 bottom: Angela Weiss/AFP/Getty Images; 2 top: AP Photo/Gregory Payan; 2 bottom: Reuters/Lucas
Jackson; 3 top: Reuters/David Ake; 3 bottom: Reuters/Paul Connors; 4 top and bottom: Reuters/Jeff
Haynes; 5 top: AP Photo/Ed Reinke; 5 bottom: Scott Utterback/Courier Journal; 6 top: Reuters/
Matt Sullivan; 6 bottom: Robert Hanashiro USATS; 7 top: AP Photo/Mark J. Terrill; 7 center: John
Reed USATS; 7 bottom, 8: AP Photo/Timothy D. Easley

ISBN 9780399563270 (hardcover)
ISBN 9780399563287 (ebook)

Printed in the United States of America
10 9 8 7 6 5 4 3 2 1

Designed by Gretchen Achilles

For Ann

CONTENTS

PROLOGUE

Imagine, for a moment, if the characters who fixed the 1919 World Series were somehow still on the scene, operating in the shadows. Arnold Rothstein, the mobster who masterminded the whole thing, was immortal—or he had finally passed on, but his sons and grandsons and various minions and flunkies still rubbed elbows with players in "chance" meetings in hotel lobbies, drank in the same bars, and befriended their friends. They insinuated themselves, latched on, and never left. There was no Kenesaw Mountain Landis, the baseball commissioner who restored faith in the honesty of the competition, but instead what remained was a lingering stain and an ongoing whiff of suspicion. The sport continued to be a source of entertainment for millions, but it went through spasms of scandal every decade or two, and there was always the feeling that another one was coming around. If you followed baseball, you did so with a degree of skepticism.

This is the history and current reality of college basketball. The sport has never been clean. It is an intimate game played on a small space with just five players a side, and it breeds relationships of all kinds, including unsavory ones. It was a magnet, right from the start, for gamblers, hustlers, and cons. City folks mostly, on the fringes of a city game.

Basketball's original sin is the practice of point shaving—the manipulation of scoring margins by players working at the direction of gamblers who have bet the point spread. The way it works is that competitors on a team favored to win, say, by 11 points, ease up enough to make sure they prevail by just eight. (They don't want to cut it too close.) They can still win the game, while the sharpies collect on their bets. It is a scheme so well suited to basketball that it grew up right along with the sport itself.

Point shaving is said to date at least as far back as the pre-NBA Boston Celtics in the 1920s, just three decades after James Naismith nailed peach baskets to the walls of the gym at the Springfield, Massachusetts, YMCA, and episodes of it have toppled major college programs and ended or curtailed the careers of some of the game's greatest players. The most famous of them was Connie Hawkins, an electric, high-flying player who was considered the Julius Erving or Michael Jordan of his day—but who lost his college career in the early 1960s and was banned by the NBA until he was twenty-seven years old.

There have been periodic outbreaks in the decades since, with prosecutions of gamblers and players connected to betting schemes at Boston College (1978), Tulane (1985), and Arizona State (1994). There is no reason to believe that point shaving does not still endure somewhere within the college basketball system.

On September 26, 2017, just days before practices for a new season were to begin, college basketball experienced its biggest jolt since a coast-to-coast wave of point shaving nearly brought the whole sport down more than half a century ago. Standing at a lectern in a federal courthouse in lower Manhattan, law enforcement officials revealed that the FBI had been investigating "the criminal influence of money on coaches and student-athletes who participate in intercollegiate basketball" for more than two years. The FBI had used its customary methods—wiretaps, hidden cameras, and criminal suspects flipped and turned into informants—to explore the sport's murky depths, down into layers that insiders would not want anyone to see. "We're talking in the realm of hundreds of calls . . . consensually recorded meetings, some videotaped meetings, probably a couple of dozen of those," a prosecutor explained. Ten people were arrested, including assistant coaches at four major programs.

The sprawling federal case involved recruiting, but the root cause was the same as what has plagued college basketball from the beginning: the big money coursing through it, now billions of dollars, that bypasses the unpaid workforce. Amateurism has long been a luxury of the upper classes. Many college basketball players come from the lower end of the socioeconomic scale, and some from outright poverty. They are easily tempted, easily compromised, and easily persuaded to break rules that some (though perhaps a dwindling few) hold sacred.

"We have your playbook," an FBI official said, indicating that the bureau would continue to fan out in the recruiting world. But what was revealed even on that first day was seismic. It put names and faces to long-rumored dirty dealing on the grassroots basketball circuit, also known as AAU basketball—the web of youth teams, sponsored by major shoe and sports apparel companies, that attract the top players and the most avid recruiting. (AAU stands for Amateur Athletic Union—though what occurs under its aegis mocks traditional definitions of amateurism.)

"Grassroots" is a catchall term that encompasses the AAU teams, their tournaments and all-star events, as well as the summer camps sponsored by the major shoe companies. An NCAA blue-ribbon panel referred to it as "ungoverned space"—as if describing a Third World conflict zone under the loose control of rival warlords. Grassroots basketball has replaced high school ball as the primary recruiting ground of college coaches. It is where players are scouted, ranked, flattered, and offered a range of benefits.

In conversations secretly taped by the FBI, college assistant coaches talk like gangsters as they accept bribes in return for setting their players up with shady agents and money managers, whose goal is to cement business relationships for when the players reach the NBA. "The motherfucker that's scoring 22 points a game" is how one coach describes a player, before promising to "bury" any rival advisor who tries to get close to the kid. One of the hustlers talks of the value of buying off coaches, explaining that they provide "complete access to a kid because if the coach says nobody can come around—can't nobody fucking come around."

Two of the defendants charged by prosecutors were connected to Adidas, one of the three major companies that contend for the loyalty of teenage players (the others are Nike and Under Armour). Prosecutors alleged that an Adidas employee and consultant created "sham invoices" to generate money for bribes and provided tens of thousands of dollars in cash that were exchanged with players' parents in hotel-room handoffs. The money was intended to induce their sons to commit to Adidas-sponsored college teams.

Basketball recruiting, or at least the periphery of it, has long been known as an unscrupulous business, a subculture populated by men dedicated to getting their hooks into young athletic flesh and working it for profit. Many people knew that the shoe companies exert an unhealthy influence. The government's focus on the rivalry between Adidas, Nike, and Under Armour makes them seem like competing crime families, and it highlights a less familiar element of the recruiting landscape—the corporatization of street-level sleaze.

Brian Bowen Jr. was a known commodity on the grassroots circuit from the time he was in his early teens—a kid who was sure to be an object of intense recruiting, sure to play at the major college level, and maybe become a pro if he kept improving. He was from Saginaw, Michigan, an economically depressed Rust Belt city with one of the highest rates of violent crime in the nation, but a basketball hotbed. Draymond Green, an all-star with the Golden State Warriors, is one of several NBA players who hail from Saginaw, where players take pride in their scrappy, physical style of play, not unlike Tom Izzo's Michigan State teams, who play just an hour to the south.

Bowen did not come away hardened by his environment, either by Saginaw or its tough-edged basketball tradition. Just the opposite. There was a sweetness about him, a shy smile and an engaging manner. He was given a nickname at birth, "Tugs," because he pulled on his mother's hair with his tiny fingers, and that was what his family, friends, teammates, and coaches called him ever since.

He played Little League baseball when he was younger, and ran track and played soccer up until eighth grade. He was an only child, and his mother chauffeured him around, fed him, and made his schedule. Even after he reached high school age, she could sometimes be seen kneeling or sitting on the bottom row of a set of bleachers as she laced up his sneakers before a game—like a figure-skating mom tightening the laces of her child's skates. In his spare time, he liked building elaborate structures with Legos. The worst that people said about Tugs was that he could seem a little sheltered.

By the time Bowen reached twelfth grade, he was six foot seven. He had played at a couple of different high schools and for several AAU teams. Like many of his peers, he was a free agent at a young age, always open to better opportunities.

As some of the nation's most famous college basketball coaches called him, texted him, sent him letters, and attended his games, Tugs let his father, Brian Bowen Sr., respond to his suitors and help him winnow them to a list of contenders. The family also brought an advisor into their circle: Christian Dawkins, a Saginaw native whose own father had been Draymond Green's high school coach.

Dawkins was young, still in his early twenties, but he knew dozens of college coaches, and even NBA scouts and general managers. Tugs trusted him. He figured Dawkins could guide him—let him know how to sort out the good guys from the bad guys.

There is a long buildup to a vaunted high school prospect finally choosing a college. It's an event. A culmination. A basketball bar mitzvah. Some prospects make the announcement in their high school gyms, in front of the whole school with ESPN broadcasting live. When Romeo Langford, a coveted prospect in the 2018 class from New Albany, Indiana, announced his decision, Indiana, his fans began lining up outside the gym at 2:30 p.m. for the big reveal—four hours before the doors opened.

Tugs let his recruitment drag on for a very long time, way past when other top recruits had committed, and then finally revealed his choice in a more low-key way, on Twitter. "Happy to announce my commitment to The Ville," he tweeted under his handle, @20Tugs, signaling that he was signing with the University of Louisville. His father followed up with a tweet of his own. "Congrats, Tugs," he wrote. "God has blessed you."

E ight college basketball programs feature prominently in the government's case: Arizona, Miami, Oklahoma State, the University of Southern California, Auburn, North Carolina State, Kansas, and Louisville. More than a dozen others have been mentioned in news reports because either their coaches or players they were recruiting came into contact with the defendants.

The consequences for most of them—the coaches, their teams and universities—are not yet fully known. But one school, the University of Louisville, is where the impact of the scandal, and its broader significance for college athletics and the future of the NCAA, can be felt and observed now.

Louisville figured out how to monetize basketball better than any other university in America. It sold hard liquor in its NBA-quality arena and marketed high-dollar premium seats and luxury boxes to affluent Louisvillians. The U. of L., as it is known locally, not only made more money on its basketball team than any other school in the NCAA, it wasn't even close: Louisville was out in front by $7 million.

A visionary athletic director, Tom Jurich, leveraged the success of the basketball team and its charismatic Hall of Fame coach, Rick Pitino, to elevate the rest of the athletic program. He raised money with ease and built stadiums, arenas, ballparks, and practice facilities, all situated on the campus's eastern edge and faced in handsome red brick. The football stadium was renovated and expanded once, then a second time, then a third. A coach who played a winning, exciting style of football helped fill the seats. Against all odds, Louisville used a series of middling conferences as stepping-stones to climb all the way up into the powerhouse Atlantic Coast Conference, alongside bluebloods Duke, North Carolina, and Virginia.

For most of its history, Louisville was an ugly duckling of a commuter school. The athletic facilities that Jurich built became known as the university's "front porch"—what it showed to the world. Sports itself was the leading edge of the U. of L. The university had successful teams across the whole program and high-achieving individual athletes. A U. of L. swimmer won an Olympic gold medal in the 2016 Summer Games in Rio de Janeiro, just two decades past a time when her university could barely afford to put chlorine in the pool.

The rest of the university followed along. It was beautified, and students moved into newly built dormitories. There was life after dark: a bar and a restaurant scene, some music venues. Other markers began to point up: The test scores of incoming freshmen. Fundraising for academics. Tuition.

Louisville was an example of how to build an institution of higher learning out of an athletic program. Right up until the moment when it became the prototype of how the whole thing blows apart.

CHAPTER ONE

FAMILY

On a late August evening in 2017, Tom Jurich, the University of Louisville's athletic director, welcomed several hundred benefactors to the annual 50 Yard Line Dinner. It was a sit-down affair held on a terrace overlooking the south end zone at Papa John's Cardinal Stadium, densely staffed, with waiters circling to quickly fill up empty wineglasses. Jurich's guests were his program's most generous donors, a cross section of the city's elite: thoroughbred breeders, coal executives, lawyers, doctors, bourbon distillers, lobbyists who worked in Frankfort, the state capital.

At sixty-one years old, Jurich had a sort of Chamber of Commerce look—short gray-flecked hair, bushy eyebrows, a barrel chest. He himself was one of Louisville's barons. The state-funded university listed his annual salary as $514,000, but if you counted the various bonuses, escalator clauses, life insurance policies, and fringes like car allowances and country club memberships, he had actually made more than $5 million the previous year. The university even threw in $30,000 for a financial planner to help him handle his money. For good measure, they calculated his tax liability and provided extra money to pay what he owed—which was referred to as "grossing up" his salary.

Jurich had taken over as athletic director in 1997, when Louisville was still largely a commuter school occupying an unprepossessing stretch of 345 acres just south of the city's downtown. The institution, one of the first colleges west of the Allegheny Mountains, dates back to 1798, but its new buildings were concrete, Brutalist structures. The campus was poorly lit, signage was just about nonexistent, and grass and weeds sprouted up through cracked walkways. The local line was that athletes on recruiting visits were brought on to campus at night and then quickly whisked back home in the morning before they could take in the full measure of the dreary surroundings. Most of the academic departments struggled to rise to mediocrity. Affluent Louisville families sent their children to Kentucky's flagship university, eighty miles east in Lexington—or out of state. To the extent that the University of Louisville was known nationally, it was for basketball and the two national championships won in the 1980s under coach Denny Crum, but even that program was in decline.

Jurich had worked as athletic director at his alma mater, Northern Arizona University, and then at Colorado State. He was a former college football player and low-round NFL draft choice married to a former Miss Wyoming. Nothing in his background suggested the breadth of his vision or the magnitude of the success he would achieve. He sensed a potential at Louisville, a hunger among the city's moneyed class for a big-time sports program and a willingness on their part to pay for it. He was a genius at forging relationships and understanding what his partners wanted. ESPN, for example, needed midweek programming. In Jurich, they found someone who would have let his student-athletes compete at 3 a.m., any day of the week, if they could be on national TV in their Cardinal red. He considered himself a "coach whisperer" and had a knack for identifying young assistants from elsewhere who could step into top jobs and elevate Louisville teams to prominence.

On the night of the dinner, the football stadium was in the midst of a $63 million expansion—following a $75 million renovation a decade before. Jurich had recently flown with John Schnatter (Papa John, the namesake of the stadium) to Dallas on Schnatter's private jet, where they were given a tour of the Cowboys' stadium by team owner Jerry Jones in order to get a better idea of how to make Louisville's facility feel like a proper football palace.

All along Floyd Street were the other facilities Jurich built, new or renovated stadiums for baseball, lacrosse, and track and field. A gleaming natatorium for the swimmers. The Trager Field Hockey Complex. (Anyone could build a field hockey stadium; Jurich constructed a *complex*.) Nearly every building carried the name of its patron, and nearly every one housed a nationally significant team—a contender for conference and NCAA championships. (Off campus, on the bank of the Ohio River, was the KFC Yum! Center, built with $238 million in public money—for the benefit of Louisville basketball.) To the extent that all of this was the university's front porch, an advertisement for the new University of Louisville, it was a little like having to walk through a Las Vegas casino, past the slots and blackjack tables, to reach your hotel room: It let you know what was important.

Jurich had many more acolytes than critics in Louisville, but he was blunt and given to bursts of anger, and some considered him a bully. At the very least, he was a bulldozer, a determined and relentless builder—a Robert Moses of college sport. He had a big announcement to make that night, another step forward for Louisville sports, and was waiting for the right moment to reveal it. He controlled the seating and had put himself at the head table along with Mitch McConnell, the Senate majority leader and a Louisville graduate; Matt Bevin, Kentucky's governor; and Junior Bridgeman, a Louisville basketball legend turned multimillionaire businessman. They were joined by two executives of Adidas.

The university had a new interim president, Gregory Postel, a radiologist turned administrator who had come over from the medical school. But he was seated away from the podium at a table with executives from Thornton's, a Louisville-based gas and convenience store chain. People noticed, and they understood the message being delivered. "Jurich wanted to let him know who the motherfucking king was," said local radio host Terry Meiners. "He relegated Postel to commoner status. When you look back on it now, it was stupid as hell."

Rick Pitino, in the summer of 2017, was on the cusp of his seventeenth season as Louisville's basketball coach. He is a New Yorker by birth, which you could still clearly hear in his accent, and a wiseass by personality type. He was often accompanied in Louisville by what Jonathan Blue, a former trustee of the university, referred to as his "Sinatra-like posse." He kept late hours and had the energy of a man decades younger. If everyone rolled home late after a night out, it was not uncommon for Pitino to call one of his fellow celebrants at 6 a.m. the next day, with an idea to discuss, a conversation to pick back up, or just because he enjoyed being an irritant. If the person on the other end sounded groggy, he'd say, "Sorry, Rip Van Winkle. Go back to sleep." When Pitino had a golf date on the horizon—he was an avid golfer and played for high stakes, sometimes up to $1,000 a hole—his playing mates could count on him to begin calling a day or two in advance, just to needle them for a competitive edge.

One of his favorite expressions was, "I'm just breaking your balls." He affected an exaggerated courtliness around women, and if he was in mixed company, he'd change it to, "I'm just breaking shoes," which made no sense, but everybody got the joke, including, of course, the women.

From a distance, it could seem that Pitino had lived a charmed life. His wife, Joanne, was his high school sweetheart in Bayville, New York. When they were in their teens, she rebounded for him as he practiced his shooting, and afterward, when he was satisfied he had put up enough shots, they went to the beach or out for ice cream. They have five children and eight grandchildren. But they had a son who died at six months old of congenital heart failure. Pitino's brother-in-law and best friend, Billy Minardi, died in the World Trade Center on September 11, 2001. Another brother-in-law was hit and killed by a taxi in Manhattan.

Pitino touted his control over the Louisville basketball program, down to the smallest detail, and claimed to be aware of every morsel of information. "If one of my players has a beer in Louisville," he once said, "I know about it." His sense of control extended to off the court, where he took great pride in his ability to use connections and pull levers to help friends. "Rick's the kind of person," Terry Meiners said, "that if you told him, 'I need 100k and a helicopter,' he'd write you the check and say, 'When do you need the chopper and where do you want it to land?'"

To people who cared about college basketball, Pitino's hiring at Louisville in 2001 was astounding—in large part because the job seemed like a couple of steps down a ladder he had already ascended. Jurich had pushed out Crum and appointed himself as a "one-man search committee" to find a replacement. He set his sights on just one candidate, Pitino, who had been a boy wonder of a head coach and was handed his first team, at Boston University, at age twenty-five. In his next college job, he led little Providence College on a miraculous run to the 1987 Final Four.

He had not only spent time in the NBA but made stops in two of its most important markets—as head coach of the New York Knicks and head coach and president of the Boston Celtics. What made his move to Louisville truly shocking was that he had already coached in Kentucky—but in Lexington, at the University of Kentucky, which he once referred to as "Camelot" and where he had a successful eight-season run that included three Final Four appearances and a national championship. He said after accepting the Louisville job that he had been close to signing with Michigan, a more prestigious university and job. When asked what stopped him, he said, "Cowardice. I can't get on the phone and tell Tom no. I can't tell him this."

Not many people remember ever talking with the single-minded Jurich about anything but Louisville sports. He did one thing and he did it extremely well. Pitino could hold forth on wine, food, and politics. (He didn't much advertise it in Kentucky, but he is a Democrat.) He had long enjoyed going to the track, but in Kentucky, home of Churchill Downs, Keeneland, and dozens of breeding farms, he became an aficionado. He invested in ownership shares of Thoroughbreds and had one that reached the Kentucky Derby. While he was still coaching in Lexington, he sometimes took recruits and their families to nearby Claiborne Farm to pay homage to the retired Secretariat.

Pitino didn't attend the 50 Yard Line Dinner. (He was the only coach at Louisville who habitually skipped it.) That August, he was within weeks of turning sixty-five, and his friends had planned a surprise party at a restaurant near his $2 million home, in a golf course community east of town. He owned a much larger house, worth about $25 million, on a private island off the coast of Miami, where his neighbors included Julio Iglesias and the investor Carl Icahn. He had tickets to go with Joanne and three other couples to an upcoming Bruno Mars concert at the Yum Center. He owned a box upstairs, but they would sit up front, in floor seats just a couple of rows from the stage.

The first full practice with his 2017–18 squad was just a little more than a month off and he was eager to get started. For all his wide interests and urbane veneer, Pitino at his core was a basketball coach—a man who showed up for work at his $8-million-a-year-job in sneakers and a warm-up suit and with a whistle around his neck. The practice gym was where he lived, and it was not hard to make an argument that he was the best college coach of his generation— the tactical and motivational genius you would want on the sideline if you needed to win just one crucial game.

No one who wins in college basketball does so without talented players, but Pitino succeeded with demonstrably less of them than his counterparts at other major programs. In sixteen years at the helm, he took his Louisville squads to three Final Fours and one national championship. Three other times, his teams fell just one game short of the Final Four. Teams that go deep into the tournament almost always have future NBA players on the roster, and Final Four mainstays like Duke, Kansas, and Kentucky have rosters perennially stocked with multiple NBA lottery picks. But during Pitino's tenure as the Cardinals' coach, just seven of his players were chosen in the NBA's first round, and none were ever among the first ten picks. His highest pick, Terrence Williams, chosen eleventh overall in 2009, played sparingly in four NBA seasons before washing out of the league and signing on with a pro team in Venezuela. (The ten seasons between 2005 and 2014 encompassed Pitino's peak years at Louisville—three Final Fours, and two seasons in which his team was stopped in the Elite Eight. In that whole decade of high achievement, he had just three first-round picks.)

High school basketball prospects are ranked by recruiting services with a system of stars, with the best of them categorized as five-star players. Pitino landed just a handful of those players over the years. His best player in recent seasons was Donovan Mitchell, one of the top two rookies in the NBA in the 2017–18 season. But Mitchell, who plays for the Utah Jazz, was only the thirteenth pick in the NBA draft, and coming out of high school, not all the scouting services had him ranked as a five-star prospect.

Pitino's overall "class rankings," the strength of his recruited players in a given year, sometimes edged into the top ten among NCAA Division I programs, but one year he was ranked as low as ninety-fourth, and another year, seventy-ninth. It is reasonable to wonder why more top players didn't want to play for Pitino—or why their parents and coaches did not want them to—but what he accomplished with the talent he assembled was a measure of his coaching acumen.

"There are certain people who are just born to lead, and Coach Pitino is one of them," says Herb Sendek, a veteran head coach who was a Pitino assistant at Providence and Kentucky. "He is a brilliant communicator who through the words he chooses and his inflection is able to transmit his own self-confidence to everyone around him. I never had any doubt, as a member of his staff, that we were going to win. He could have been anything he wanted—the CEO of a company, a governor, or a high-ranking military leader."

There's not a coach in big-time college basketball whose program is totally pure. It's not possible. But Pitino came to Louisville relatively clean, with just one blemish on his record—NCAA violations from way back in the mid-1970s when he was an assistant, and then briefly the interim head coach, at the University of Hawaii. At Louisville, though, he survived two tawdry, embarrassing scandals.

The first one was personal in nature: a sexual assignation in a restaurant, after closing time, with a woman he had just met for the first time earlier in the same evening. The episode came to light, in great detail, after she tried to extort him and was prosecuted in federal court—with Pitino in the role of star prosecution witness.

The second scandal was even worse because it involved his players. In what became known as "Strippergate," a local escort revealed that one of Pitino's assistants had paid for parties at the basketball dormitory, where she and other women, including her daughters, danced and had sex with high school kids on recruiting visits as well as with some current players. Even though the parties went on over the course of four years, Pitino insisted that he had no knowledge of them.

Not many coaches could have emerged from the first scandal without being fired. It's possible that Pitino is the *only* one who would have survived two affairs that sordid. But he was winning games and packing Yum Center to its 22,090-seat capacity. His team was the engine of the athletic department, and to a large extent, the university itself.

The NCAA, the governing body of college sports, has a logic and lexicon all its own. It put the nude dancing performances enjoyed by Pitino's players and recruits, and the oral sex they received, in its category of "impermissible benefits." As Pitino prepared to coach in the fall of 2017, the consequences of Strippergate were still not fully known, and possibly serious sanctions from the NCAA still loomed.

Like most successful sports figures, however—coaches or players—Pitino was a champion at compartmentalizing, blocking out distractions, even ones he may have been responsible for himself. He had reason to be excited about the upcoming season. His roster was stocked with talented upperclassmen as well as a rarity, a five-star recruit—Brian Bowen Jr.

Tugs was the very last of the premium high school prospects in the class of 2017 to commit to a school, and he seemed to enjoy the speculation about where he might finally land. No one guessed Louisville, because it had not been on his list and was not among the schools Bowen traveled to in his five official visits permitted by the NCAA. The scouting services noted his fluid athleticism and sweet shooting stroke. One called him an "impact scorer," and another labeled him "loaded with potential and upside."

In addition, he had some personality and style—his bleached-blond hair was meant to mimic the 'do of NFL star Odell Beckham Jr.—and a flair for drama. He figured to help the team and delight the home crowd at the Yum Center. When he finally announced his choice, one headline read: "Bowen Once Thought Headed to Michigan State or Arizona, but Louisville Comes out of Nowhere."

Even Pitino said he was shocked. He couldn't believe his good fortune! In his telling, Bowen's decision was a gift that fell from the heavens, like one of those letters informing a recipient of some large sum of money left by a distant relative. "We got lucky on this one," he said. "They had to come in unofficially, pay for their hotel, pay for their meals. We spent zero dollars recruiting a five-star athlete who I loved when I saw him play. In my forty years of coaching, this is the luckiest I've been."

After the entrees at the 50 Yard Line Dinner were served (suitably manly options of filet or stuffed peppers with shrimp), Jurich stood up to acknowledge Jim Murphy and Chris McGuire, the Adidas executives at his table. The university was already in business with the German-based company, which provided uniforms and other gear for its teams and annual cash payments to the athletic program. In return, Adidas got exposure for its brand every time a Louisville team played—and carte blanche entree to the university's students, to alumni, and to greater Louisville. If you walked into the campus bookstore, you encountered racks and racks of Adidas-branded Louisville product—a sea of red hoodies, warm-up pants, T-shirts, gym bags, clothes for children and babies—before you came across an actual book. At Louisville's airport, arriving passengers exiting the secure area walked under a giant University of Louisville banner overlaid with an Adidas logo and the slogan "It Is Here, the Future of Sport Will Be Written."

Apparel deals, as they're called, are celebrated as co-branding opportunities, marriages between institutions of higher learning and sneaker companies even as they turn college athletes, who are ostensibly amateurs, into human billboards. For college sports coaches and executives, they are another way to compete and keep score. In 2016, after the University of California at Los Angles set a new standard for apparel deals, a fifteen-year, $260 million contract with Under Armour, the school's football coach, Jim Mora Jr., said, "That resonates with a recruit or a parent. They'll think, 'UCLA is really becoming big, big, big time.'"

UCLA, of course, is already a college of some note. It is ranked among the nation's best public universities and has produced seven Nobel Prize winners over its century-long history—as well as the greatest dynasty in the annals of college sports, the ten NCAA basketball championships won by John Wooden–led teams in the 1960s and 1970s. To Mora, however, what really put the university on the map was the imprimatur of Under Armour, a Baltimore-based upstart whose founder began selling compression shorts out of the trunk of his car in 1996.

Louisville's existing contract with Adidas was modest and not in line with its new status. It was signed before Pitino's national championship in 2013, before the football team pulled off a huge upset in the Sugar Bowl that same year, defeating third-ranked Florida—and before the school jumped several classes and was accepted into the Atlantic Coast Conference, one of the NCAA's "Power Five," after years of bouncing between such low-wattage confederations as Conference USA and the Metro Conference. The new Louisville was a legitimate all-sports superpower, and it was deserving, in the calculus of college athletics, of rich deals with its corporate patrons.

After introducing the Adidas executives, Jurich announced that the university's contract with the company was being extended and sweetened. Adidas was signing on to sponsor Louisville athletics for another ten years in return for $160 million in cash and apparel. It was the largest contract Adidas had signed with any university, and the fourth richest in the nation, putting Louisville behind only UCLA's Under Armour deal and Nike's agreements with Ohio State and Texas. There were a couple of loud whoops in the crowd, and everyone rose to their feet and cheered as if the home team had just kicked a game-winning field goal.

At a press conference on the morning after the dinner, Jurich announced the Adidas deal publicly and stressed that the close relationship between Louisville and its apparel partner was about more than money. "We're part of the Adidas family and I certainly hope they know that they are part of the Cardinal family," he said. "This is not something that we say, 'We can give you some more signage. Or we can give you some more airtime. Or we can give you TV commercials.' This is something that they are going to be a part of our life, and a way of life."

One month later, federal agents arrested James Gatto, an Adidas executive and the company's main point of contact with the grassroots basketball scene—the incubator for top prospects—and charged him with conspiring to pay bribes to induce high school stars to sign with Adidas-sponsored universities. The investigation, conducted by the FBI and overseen by the U.S. Attorney's office for the Southern District of New York, reached up into the very highest levels of college basketball and NCAA sports. In doing so, it reduced the vaunted program built by Tom Jurich to the status of a perp.

Documents filed by federal prosecutors identified a focus of their inquiry as "University-6"—"a public research institution located in Kentucky with approximately 22,640 students." A top player who signed with its basketball team late in the recruiting season, and seemingly out of the blue, was "Player-10." The man who would coach this surprise recruit was "Coach-2." All of this was easily and instantly decoded by journalists and others with a knowledge of college basketball and recruiting. The university was Louisville. The player, Brian Bowen Jr. The coach, Rick Pitino. Pitino has not been charged with any crime, nor has Brian Bowen Jr.

Christian Dawkins was one of the ten individuals charged. He is alleged to have been a conduit between Adidas and Brian Bowen Jr.'s father, as well as the link to several other players and college coaches. According to the criminal complaint, Bowen chose to enroll at Louisville after Dawkins, Gatto, and others agreed to funnel $100,000 to his father.

Dawkins's words, captured on the FBI recordings, can be taken as something like a tutorial on the dark underworld of college recruiting. He instructs associates at various points on how to conceal payments to players or their families, sometimes by routing them through the bank accounts of the nonprofit youth teams they play for. The government alleged that Dawkins's goal, and the aim of several others in the conspiracy, was not just to direct players to certain schools, but to put themselves in a favored position once (and if) those players reached the NBA. The bribes were down payments on future revenue. "If we take care of everybody and everything is done, we control everything," the government quoted Dawkins as saying at one secretly recorded meeting. "You can make millions off of one kid."

———

Twenty-four hours after the FBI and U.S. Attorney's office announced the arrests and the dimensions of the criminal case at a press conference in Manhattan, Rick Pitino was removed as Louisville's basketball coach. It was an abrupt, ignominious exit. He was locked out of his office and denied access to his email. A letter sent to him by the administration explained that the action was made necessary by "your conduct over a period of years" and "a pattern and practice of inappropriate behavior." The pattern, of course, was long-standing and not exactly a secret.

Pitino called his wife and told her to quickly pack a bag and meet him at the airport, where they would fly on a private plane to Miami. He vowed never to return to Kentucky except in the case of one eventuality—if one of his horses again qualified for the Kentucky Derby.

Brian Bowen Jr. was immediately separated from the Louisville basketball team. As his would-be teammates began practice, under a thirty-two-year-old interim coach elevated to step in for Pitino, he pushed himself through lonely workouts in a church gym about twenty minutes north of campus. It wasn't at all clear that Bowen Jr. ever saw any of the cash—it may have just gone to his father—or if he even knew of any deal.

Tom Jurich, too, was fired. He had not only stood by Pitino through two previous scandals but had steadfastly defended other coaches when their jobs were under threat, including a women's lacrosse coach accused of abusive behavior. The letter terminating Jurich said that he had failed to properly supervise coaches and engaged in "willful misconduct." It was signed by "Gregory C. Postel,

M.D."—the interim president and the guy he had put in the cheap seats at the 50 Yard Line Dinner.

It should be noted that the university was at that point due for a reckoning. The place, charitably, was a mess. In the previous year, its full board of trustees had been removed by Kentucky's governor and replaced with new trustees, then reinstated when a judge said the action was not done properly, and then fired and replaced again after the governor figured out how to do it legally. An independent audit found that the upper level of the university's administration was a swamp of self-dealing and secret payouts, with tens of millions of dollars going to dubious real estate transactions and to massive raises for insiders meant to be invisible to the public. The university's accrediting body, the Southern Association of Colleges and Schools, was concerned enough about the institution's inability to govern itself that it put Louisville on probation.

Not all of the school's problems were caused by its vaunted athletic program. But none of them were unrelated to it. The university made a big bet on sports. It doubled and tripled down. The recruiting scandal and the firing of Jurich and Pitino equated to a whole big pile of chips getting swept off the gaming table.

In exile in Florida, Pitino was raging and defiant. His empire was gone, his legacy stained. His teams had always scratched and clawed and were miserable to play against. They *competed*. Every game, right to the end. Why wouldn't anyone do that for him?

He looked around at other head coaches implicated in the scandal and wondered why they still had their jobs. He had not been criminally charged, and neither had any of his assistant coaches—though one of them was caught on videotape in a meeting with

Dawkins in a Las Vegas hotel room. He figured it all would have passed, like other crises in his life had, if Louisville had been willing to just dig in and fight. He felt like everyone had given up while there was still time left on the clock.

"You fire the head coach and you send a red flag to the NCAA that Louisville did some things wrong," he said. "They told the whole country I was guilty. Everybody else in the country stayed calm and said, 'Wait a minute. What's all this about?'"

CHAPTER TWO

FOOTPRINTS

With his ten NCAA championships in the 1960s and 1970s, his innovative methods, and his mentorship of such stars as Kareem Abdul-Jabbar and Bill Walton, the late UCLA coach John Wooden is college basketball's most revered figure. The John R. Wooden Award goes to the nation's top player each year. The basketball court at UCLA's iconic Pauley Pavilion is named for Wooden. In 2003, President George W. Bush honored Wooden, then ninety-two, with the Presidential Medal of Freedom, the nation's highest civilian honor.

But in addition to being the greatest coach in the game's history, Wooden is the prototype for every coach since who has tried to cover himself in a cloak of deniability. On the day after he died in 2010, the *Los Angeles Times* wrote, "If Wooden was the father figure of UCLA basketball, Gilbert was its shadowy one." The reference was to Sam Gilbert, a builder in Los Angeles who was close to Wooden's players. An investigative series the paper published in 1981 called Gilbert a "one-man clearinghouse" who helped players get cars, clothes, airline tickets, scalpers' prices for tickets, and even, on occasion, abortions for their girlfriends. A former NCAA investigator said he had looked into Gilbert's involvement and "could have put UCLA on indefinite probation" but was told to drop his case.

Even back when the story was published, it was not exactly news to the basketball cognoscenti—Gilbert's relationship to the UCLA program had been an open secret—and the allegations were not startling to Wooden. The newspaper wrote that Wooden was wary of Gilbert but generally turned a blind eye. (Gilbert was indicted in 1987 on racketeering charges by prosecutors, who were not aware that he had died four days earlier. The case centered on a marijuana smuggling ring and was unrelated to his involvement with UCLA basketball.) "Maybe I had tunnel vision. I still don't think he's had any great impact on the basketball program," Wooden commented a half dozen years after he had retired. He seemed to argue that it may be better not to know certain things. "There's as much crookedness as you want to find. There was something Abraham Lincoln said—he'd rather trust and be disappointed than distrust and be miserable all the time. Maybe I trusted too much."

The two reporters who worked on the series, Mike Littwin and Alan Greenberg, would later write, "Wooden knew about Gilbert. He knew the players were close to Gilbert. He knew they looked to Gilbert for advice. Maybe he knew more. He should have known much more. If he didn't, it was only because he apparently chose not to look."

Pitino has said numerous times in the wake of his downfall that the rule-breaking uncovered by the FBI is nothing new and has been going on for years. Wooden's career in college coaching was just ending as his started, but Pitino is enough of a historian of the game to know that it dates to the era of the storied UCLA coach—and, indeed, to well before that.

It is hard to imagine now, but in the years before World War II and into the early 1950s, Long Island University was a national power in college basketball, the UCLA of its era. Its team won the National Invitation Tournament, in Madison Square Garden, in 1939 and 1941, when the NIT was a far more important event than the NCAA tourney, and LIU had one winning streak of 43 games, another of 38. Its coach, Clair Bee, wrote the introduction to James Naismith's only book on basketball, mentored a young Bobby Knight, and was an early proponent of the NBA's 24-second shot clock. When he died in 1983, the *New York Daily News* sports columnist Mike Lupica wrote, "The story of the old man's life is merely the history of basketball in this country."

But Bee's career, fittingly, is also the history of basketball scandal. Three members of his 1950–51 team were convicted for conspiring with gamblers to shave points. One of them was his best player, Sherman White, that season's consensus player of the year. The LIU captain from the previous season, Eddie Gard, helped set up the scheme, and White, who would serve nine months in prison at Rikers Island, said that point shaving had been endemic at LIU for a generation and that players were schooled on how to get the required result. "You don't do it on offense," he said. "You had to keep your rhythm on offense. You had to do it on defense. You had to turn your head or you had to slide and let a guy go in to make a basket."

First, the scandal touched other basketball powers in New York at the time—New York University, Manhattan College, and City College of New York—and then what was termed the "fix virus" swept into the Midwest and all the way to the West Coast. It hit Adolph Rupp's famed Kentucky team, and the school shut down his program for the 1952–53 season. LIU would drop its basketball program for a half dozen years; the team never returned to national prominence.

The judge in Sherman White's trial, Saul Streit of the New York State Supreme Court, "blamed Bee, other coaches, and college administrators for creating a highly commercialized climate that contributed to the young men's corruption," wrote Dennis Gildea, a biographer of Bee. The judge made those remarks almost seventy years ago, when the level of money and commercialization in college sports was a trickle compared to what it is today. Then, as now, very little of the money ever flowed to the players. If they got anything at all it was usually not much more than pocket change—but it was enough for them to give in to the temptation and more than enough to wreck their futures.

There are parallels between that era and almost every aspect of college sports today. The money was smaller, but the essence of the transactions—young players used as pawns in the grand schemes of their elders—was the same.

Like today's recruiting scandals, point shaving in the 1940s and 1950s was an open secret. Insiders knew exactly how it worked and sometimes recognized it in real time. Gildea writes of a scene after

LIU defeated Bowling Green at Madison Square Garden in 1951 but let an 18-point lead dwindle to a 6-point victory, which was inside the point spread. Clair Bee met a couple of sportswriter friends at a Midtown bar afterward, their custom back then, and one of the writers said to him, "Your team just dumped a game."

Bee would have a second act as the author of the popular Chip Hilton series of sports books for adolescent readers—twenty-one volumes that he first started writing while still at LIU. His hero, Chip, played for a fictional team known as "State" and was always faced with some kind of moral or ethical dilemma, but he was incorruptible. Chip not only unfailingly did the right thing, but he also convinced his teammates to keep it on the up-and-up. He was the straight-arrow figure that Bee wished he had coached.

Many considered Bee's literary efforts to be, consciously or not, an attempt to expiate himself for his role as the coach of a dirty team. He was the model of a modern coach in his response to scandal, meaning that he presented himself as a tower of rectitude who was blindsided by his players' wrongdoing. What he knew or should have known—or actively sought not to know—has never been clear.

In some of the more recent point-shaving cases, gambling allegations have been interlaced with evidence of recruiting violations. And why wouldn't that be the case? The two versions of rule-breaking occur in the same context: Players come to believe, or are convinced by others, that they deserve some of the bounty of the sport. (One of the players involved in the 1985 Tulane point-shaving case said that he had accepted $10,000 to commit to the university—given to him in cash, in a shoebox.)

Major college basketball and football programs currently generate revenue of more than $4 billion. That is just what accrues directly to the schools and the NCAA. It does not include, to give just one example, the more than $10 billion wagered annually on the NCAA basketball tournament.

In sentencing players involved in Arizona State's 1994 gambling episode, the judge said, "The scandal leads to cynicism about what college sports is all about." But you could easily make a different argument—that rule-breaking in college sports is less the cause than the consequence of long-standing and deep-seated cynicism. Cheating is what occurs when the rules are not enforced and when no one takes them seriously.

I n the post-Wooden era, the money and benefits directed to young basketball players began to be systematized. There were still sugar daddies on the scene, well-connected boosters like Sam Gilbert, but much of the largesse directed to top prospects now had a common source: Nike and the other shoe and apparel companies. Some of it is doled out in ways that, at least technically, are permissible under NCAA guidelines—for example, the boxes of shoes and athletic gear that begin flooding into the homes of promising young players while they are still in grade school. Or the generous donations that flow to their AAU programs—to teams that are sometimes run by their fathers, uncles, relatives, or close family friends.

There is no disagreement about who put the shoe companies in control of so many levers of the sport. That person is Sonny Vaccaro. If Wooden is the most venerated figure in the history of college basketball, Vaccaro is the most complicated. He has been at various points in his career a corrupting influence and a clarifying one. A bullshitter and a truth-teller.

Vaccaro was born about a year before the United States entered World War II and grew up in the western Pennsylvania town of Trafford, about thirty minutes east of Pittsburgh. He was a good enough baseball player to be drafted by the Pirates. He chose to play college football, but got hurt, washed out of two college football programs, and spent a couple of decades knocking around different locales and careers. He was briefly an assistant basketball coach at Wichita State, a rock music promoter, and a card player in Las Vegas. The authors of *Sole Influence,* a book published in 2000 on the impact of shoe companies in basketball, described Vaccaro in Las Vegas as a "small-time sharpie." (His younger brother Jimmy had better luck in the desert and the good sense to work for the house; he has run the sports book at several casinos, including Steve Wynn's Mirage.)

Sonny Vaccaro made his way back home and taught phys ed at his old high school. An annual all-star game he organized for the nation's best high school basketball players, called the Dapper Dan Roundball Classic, became a big hit locally—Pittsburgh at the time didn't have much going on, and the game packed the Civic Center each spring to capacity—and it put Vaccaro on a course to becoming a kingmaker in college recruiting. He was a salesman at heart, and he had found his product.

In the early 1980s, he went to work for Nike, which was then a company dedicated to selling shoes to elite track and field athletes and recreational runners. The company's founder, Phil Knight, wanted to get into the basketball business, but the sport was dominated by Converse, and had been going all the way back to World War I, when the company began producing its iconic Chuck Taylor model. Wilt Chamberlain, Bill Russell, and Jerry West wore "Chucks" when the tops were still made of canvas. When Vaccaro went to work for Nike, Magic Johnson, Larry Bird, and most of the rest of the NBA's stars were still wearing Converse.

Phil Knight wanted a prominent young player to become Nike's hoops ambassador, and Vaccaro convinced him that it should be Michael Jordan—over the objections of some in the company who thought the choice should be Charles Barkley or Hakeem Olajuwon, both of whom, like Jordan, came out of college and entered the NBA in 1984.

Jordan, of course, validated Vaccaro's acumen as a talent scout. On the court he was electric; off it, he was a charismatic pitchman with a made-for-TV smile. The commercials produced for Nike, especially the early ones made by Spike Lee, with "Mars Blackmon" as Lee's alter ego, permeated the culture. The Nike-manufactured Air Jordans were a triumph as a performance basketball shoe and a style tour de force. It all worked magically. Without Vaccaro, Jordan might just be another basketball star, and Nike a company that made running shoes.

Vaccaro is best known for bringing Jordan to Nike, but two other of his innovations have had an equally powerful impact, and they relate directly to the current recruiting scandal. Nike and other companies had been giving away free shoes to prominent college programs as a way to boost the company's profile. Vaccaro suggested to Knight, his boss, why not *pay* college coaches to have their teams wear their shoes? It wouldn't really cost much, and since their rival companies were also giving away shoes, it would tilt the competition in their favor.

He went after the biggest names in coaching—John Thompson of Georgetown would end up on Nike's board, with several million dollars in stock—but the initial deals were modest, just $5,000 or $10,000 a coach, depending on the size and prestige of the program. Vaccaro paid the coaches out of his own pocket and then got reimbursed, because Nike had no budget for it, but the contracts were the basis for every big-money apparel deal with colleges that followed.

The deals made college basketball "bigger," a goal of all coaches and athletic directors—and it put more money in the game's pipeline. ("Bigger" in sports almost always translates to more money—and in college sports, it means more money to coaches.) The tournaments and all-star games now sponsored by the shoe companies amount to one-stop shopping for the coaches. Instead of flying from high school to high school to see one or two prospects at a time—in almost all cases, matched up against inferior competition—they attend a limited number of big events where the best players compete against one another.

And the events take place in major metropolitan areas, where the coaches can stay in five-star hotels. It was another stroke of genius by Vaccaro, who like any salesman was acutely aware of his clients' needs. He put money in coaches' pockets *and* made their lives easier.

The logic of partnerships between the shoe companies and college basketball coaches was established. They had a legitimate role on campus; all they had to do was buy their way in. Anyone who questioned it was quickly drowned out by a chorus of happy insiders, and even now, that remains the case. "Let's not go crazy here. Shoe companies have been great for our sport," Duke coach Mike Krzyzewski said in October 2017, not long after news of the federal charges broke. "Many colleges have shoe deals that fund all their student-athletes. We wouldn't have all that. They fund programs, grassroots things that help thousands and thousands of kids. Just because we've had a few things go wrong here, you can't get rid of all that."

A big part of what the shoe companies bought was obeisance. In 2012, Adidas outfitted its client teams in unconventional new uniforms for postseason play. Rather than honoring the school's traditions, they called attention to the company. Louisville, in place of its classic red, played in what Adidas called "InfraRED" jerseys, which were infused with pink and orange. "We look like highlighters," Louisville basketball player Peyton Siva said. Baylor's "Electricity" uniforms were neon yellow down to their socks and shoelaces. Adidas announced that its "Adizero" uniforms were also going to be worn by players at the McDonald's All-American Game, the annual marquee event for the most coveted high school performers.

The attention-getting uniforms brought exactly what Adidas hoped for—a flood of free media, much of it consisting of the nonsense that the tricked-up threads conferred a performance advantage. A story in *USA Today* that read like a long press release claimed the uniforms were meant to "pay homage to the high intensity of the NCAA tournament" and were "28 percent lighter" than what the teams were wearing during regular-season play. (If that was true, you had to wonder why the company had previously burdened players with overly heavy uniforms.)

An Adidas executive said, "The most important reason why we come to work is figuring out how we can give athletes a competitive advantage—make them one step quicker, jump one inch higher, and give them extra confidence." He added that he had commissioned a survey of some younger players, kids playing on an elite

AAU team, and they all liked the uniforms, and every one of them had used the word "swag" in describing them.

The following season, Adidas outfitted six schools, including Louisville and Kansas, in "camo" jerseys. They looked absurd, nothing like basketball uniforms, and the spectacle of them seemed to toughen up some of the media coverage, including in the previously fawning *USA Today*, which noted that "in the relationship between college athletics and apparel companies, the Nikes and Adidases of the world hold the cards."

Kansas coach Bill Self got right to the heart of his program's bond with its shoe and apparel sponsor. He did not enthuse over the uniforms, but explained, "Sometimes you've got to be a team player, and Adidas has certainly been good to us, there's no question. And this is something that was important to them, that they are able to market it with some other schools that they feel that can help them in this area. Certainly, we're going to do that to try to help them."

Vaccaro's other idea was to radically ratchet down the age at which he started wooing players. Why wait till the players are in college, or even high school? It doesn't take a lot of money to win the love of a middle or grade school player and his family. Just regular shipments of shoes, which might have a retail value of $100 or more but cost only a fraction of that to produce. Nike probably spent more money shipping them to young prospects than making them.

Vaccaro had zeroed in on Jordan as he was wrapping up his career at North Carolina. In 1996, after Vaccaro had split with Nike and moved on to Adidas, he signed up Kobe Bryant, who was entering the NBA directly from Lower Merion High School in suburban

Philadelphia. "I knew the family. They knew me," he explained, making it clear that he had been laying the groundwork for several years.

Vaccaro is a colorful figure, and journalists, even ones troubled by the influence he yielded, have always loved to quote him. He has a way of speaking that can make it seem like he walked right out of *The Godfather,* and he is smart and self-aware enough that it is safe to assume he has workshopped that aspect of his persona. Vaccaro gave Jim Gatto, the indicted Adidas executive, his first job in the shoe and apparel business. After the criminal charges were announced, Vaccaro said, "I know Jimmy Gatto. I hired him. An altar boy. I have known him since birth."

When I talked with Vaccaro, he expressed shock at the gullibility of everyone involved. "The most obvious thing is you never use phones," he observed. "And if you're going to do these things, don't do them with people you don't know."

There were limits, he said, that had not been observed and caution flags that must have been missed. He had stepped down from his post at Adidas in 2007, and it looked to him that in the time he was gone, the money had gotten even bigger and the competition meaner. "Everybody forgot the boundaries of what they could do with their deals. No one stopped and thought, 'What are the legal ramifications?'"

That Louisville's program was wrapped up in the federal case surprised Vaccaro. He has known Pitino for more than forty years. "Rick is Rick," he said. "He's the cute sharp dresser, the first guy to put the Armanis on, and he could coach like no one else. It would have been a hell of a lot easier if he had better guys, but he won, and he figured out how to do it with whatever talent he had."

———

Nike's association with Jordan and the incredible success of it led to a misconception—that the shoe companies are engaged in a quest to identify kids who will hit it big in the NBA. The proverbial search for the next Jordan. That may have been the case for a time, but it has not been for many years. There are about 450 NBA players at any given time, and fewer than two dozen have their own signature shoe. (Mostly the ones you would expect—LeBron James, Stephen Curry, Kevin Durant, Chris Paul, and other superstars, though a few lesser names, like Matthew Dellavedova, have signature shoes for aspiring Chinese brands Peak or Anta.)

None of them, not even LeBron James, has come close to matching the appeal of Jordan in the marketplace, whose Air Jordans, fifteen years after his retirement as an active player, accounted for $2.6 billion in sales in 2016. James's shoe sales totaled about one-eighth of that. (The person who has come the closest to Jordan in cross-cultural appeal for his sneakers is not a basketball player but a rapper, Kanye West, whose limited-edition Yeezys sell out almost instantly and then are resold for hundreds of dollars above their retail price on the secondary market.)

The real goal of the shoe companies, in their outreach to young players, is to buy brand loyalty and enter them into a pipeline that leads to the college teams they sponsor. If the players make it to the pros and rock the shoe and gear in the NBA, that's a bonus. Gear that is especially blingy may even attract players whom a college coach covets. After signing to play basketball for Oregon, Bol Bol, a top prospect in the high school class of 2018 and the son of former NBA player Manute Bol, said that what first attracted him was that the Nike-sponsored team "had a lot of jerseys, a lot of different shoe combinations."

No young player is going to solely build a brand. Jordan did that, and it was a phenomenon of basketball talent, marketing genius, and good timing that will never be replicated. "When I was with Nike I wanted a kid to go to a Nike school," Vaccaro said. "I didn't give a shit which one. Same with Adidas. Just go to some Adidas school, one where they win games and get in the tournament and get on TV. Otherwise, we could give the money to Appalachian State if we just wanted to be good guys. But it's a business deal, not a basketball deal."

The ten-year, $160 million contract that Tom Jurich signed with Adidas included in its value about $6 million a year in shoes and gear for Louisville's teams. It was explicit about what items each sport would receive, when athletes were required to wear it, under what circumstances they could obscure the company's logo (which is called "spatting"), and what financial penalties the U. of L. would incur for instances of unauthorized spatting.

Football players were getting jerseys and pants, a "base layer" to wear under the uniforms, as well as cleats, gloves, and other accessories. Men's and women's basketball players got uniform tops and bottoms and, of course, sneakers. The rest of the U. of L. teams were in line for uniforms and a variety of gear—basically, anything related to their sport that was in the Adidas line of products. All the athletes were to wear the Adidas products exclusively for practices, games, clinics, and certain other unspecified university functions. Coaches and other athletic department staff were also required to dress in Adidas-branded gear during their official duties, and nothing with the "trade name, trademark, or logo" of any other company.

Spatting refers to ankle taping, except that the tape goes around the shoe and over the sock. It is more like bracing. As many as half the players in the NFL have their ankles spatted every game. Many athletic trainers believe in it, and some studies have shown that it cuts down on the occurrence of ankle sprains, though some players may also consider it a fashion statement. Much attention was paid to the issue of spatting in the Louisville contract, as it is in most deals between universities and apparel companies. Under the terms of the agreements, the student-athletes are action figures festooned with company logos, and anything that covers up those symbols runs counter to the whole spirit of the partnerships.

The language about spatting directly inserts the companies into issues involving players' medical conditions and needs. In 2013, *USA Today* wrote about the University of California's contract with Nike and concerns that its football team might be in violation because too many players were spatting. The newspaper uncovered an email from the athletic director, Sandy Barbour, to the team's equipment manager and head athletic trainer. "I believe that even in the case of injury, we are limited in the number of shoes that may be spatted for any given game," she wrote.

The Adidas contract with Louisville called for just a warning after a "first occurrence" of unauthorized spatting, meaning without a written medical explanation, and financial penalties for a "second occurrence of spatting" and a "third occurrence of spatting." Violations for postseason games brought stiffer penalties, and Louisville under certain circumstances could lose up to 25 percent of its Adidas deal in a given year for players covering up their Adidas logos in NCAA tournament or football bowl games.

The contract states that Adidas must be advised about medical conditions of Louisville athletes requiring spatting. (It is hard to see how its language does not come into conflict with federal regulations protecting the confidentiality of individuals' health information.) "University acknowledges that 'spatting,' taping or otherwise covering up any portions of any Adidas logo or trademark on athletic footwear supplied by Adidas is inconsistent with the purpose and terms of this agreement," it says. "University agrees it will not permit such 'spatting' or taping unless it has been medically prescribed and Adidas has been so advised."

It then goes on to say that if there is a medical problem, Adidas must have an opportunity to remedy it. "In the event any team member shall at any time suffer any physical injury, pain, or discomfort attributed to the use of Adidas shoes due to a bona-fide medical condition as evidenced by a certification by the team physician which is serious enough to affect the athlete's performance, then university shall so advise Adidas and afford Adidas the opportunity to remedy the problem."

Only if Adidas cannot make its shoe fit "reasonably satisfactorily" can an athlete wear another company's shoes. But in that case, he is *required* to spat, in order to "completely cover all non-Adidas logos, trademarks and brand insignia . . . while wearing non-Adidas shoes."

Performance bonuses were written into Louisville's contract with Adidas—for the university, of course, not the players. The company pledged $300,000 for a national championship in men's basketball, $150,000 for a Final Four appearance, and $50,000 for a conference championship. Football was also promised $300,000 for a national championship, along with $100,000 for getting to the semifinal game of the Bowl Championship Series. Women's basketball would earn $200,000 for a national championship and $75,000 for playing in a Final Four.

If Adidas were to use an athlete's "name, image, likeness, avatar and/or appearance" in connection with advertising, it had to get approval from the university and follow applicable NCAA rules. (The contract does not say anything about getting the athlete's approval.)

There are a few exceptions for when athletes can openly wear competitors' gear. One is after championship games, when gear commemorating the moment seems to magically appear and players are captured on camera with broad smiles proudly wearing the T-shirts and hats they've just been handed—which are often part of a contract that the NCAA or a conference has cut with an apparel company. (In that case, for example, a Louisville player might be handed a Nike-branded hat.) In the contract, these are termed "celebration moments," during which Louisville's student-athletes are permitted to wear "celebration products," even if they come from a rival company.

CHAPTER THREE

WAITING FOR BRIAN BOWEN

As Tom Jurich worked to finalize Louisville's new contract with Adidas, Rick Pitino was still putting his team together for the 2017–18 season. By his own high standards, he was in a slump. The previous year was a rare moment when his squad underperformed. Louisville had an excellent regular season, winning home games against archrival Kentucky and vaunted Duke. They prevailed at Syracuse, an accomplishment for any visiting team. But after earning a No. 2 seed in the Midwest region, the Cardinals could not survive the first weekend of the tournament, losing to seventh-seeded Michigan.

The year before that, Louisville was ineligible for the tournament—fallout from Strippergate. The university declared that it would not compete in the postseason in hopes of avoiding even stiffer penalties from the NCAA, a common tactic known as a "self-imposed ban," but one that irritated Pitino. He thought it implied that he had done something wrong.

In the upcoming season, however, five of his top players were returning, a good base in an era of college basketball when talented underclassmen on highly ranked teams routinely enter the NBA draft. In addition, Pitino had a top-ten recruiting class coming in, one of his best in years—and that was even before Brian Bowen Jr. began to look like a possibility. Pitino, in fact, thought he was done recruiting for the year. "We've got the best recruiting class we've had in sixteen years," he said. "We got everybody we wanted."

Bowen is the son of a white mother, Carrie Malecke, and an African American father, Brian Bowen Sr., a former high school basketball star who became a cop in Saginaw. Bowen Sr. trained and mentored his nephew, Jason Richardson, when he was a promising young basketball player coming up in Saginaw. "I became what they call uncle-dad" is how Bowen described the relationship in a 2014 interview. "When Jason was twelve or thirteen, from that time, it was me and Jason."

When Richardson went off to start his freshman season at Michigan State, the Bowens moved from Saginaw to East Lansing to be near him. The move came at about the same time Bowen left the Saginaw police force with a medical disability pension. (It pays him $48,513 annually.)

East Lansing was where Tugs was born and where he became his father's next basketball project. Ball handling had been a weakness of Jason Richardson's when he was younger, so that was something

Bowen Sr. went to work on right away. "From the time he started playing, I made sure he could handle the ball with both hands," he said. "When he was eight or nine months standing against the table, I made sure he used both hands to roll a ball around and develop that ambidexterity in both hands."

Jason Richardson stayed two years at Michigan State, helping lead the Spartans to a national championship in his freshman season, before setting off on a long and lucrative NBA career. He played fourteen seasons and earned $105 million in salary. Brian Bowen Sr. sometimes traveled with Richardson in his self-described role as advisor. He moved the family back to Saginaw, where he purchased a home with a full-court basketball court in the backyard and spent thousands of hours drilling his son on fundamentals.

The court became a magnet for kids in Saginaw who were serious players. It was a place to try moves they had learned from their own basketball mentors and to test themselves against their competition for playing time on school and AAU teams. They were working, not playing, and Brian Bowen Sr. stood watch on the sideline, offering instruction and keeping the games as clean as he could. The surface was cement at first, but he tore that out and replaced it with VersaCourt, a softer, synthetic material that came in sections that fit together like puzzle pieces. "He was looking ahead even back then," his son says. "If it would have stayed cement I would have wrecked my knees and I wouldn't have been able to amount to anything."

Americans like to believe in the myth of the self-made athlete, the kid who succeeds because he just outworks everybody. But the top levels of sport are made up of those who start out with the right DNA. They are the pool of candidates for stardom—and the most focused, hardest-working, and luckiest of them rise to the top.

One reason that basketball players are scouted at such a young age—and that evaluations of them are often right—is that the universe of human beings with the height and athleticism of elite players is limited. They are oversized people with extraordinary physical dexterity. A typical guard in the NBA is between six foot three and six foot six, and the rest of the players range on up to seven feet and beyond. If a kid looks like he'll grow tall enough and is sufficiently quick and skilled—and seems to possess the grit and imagination that are the components of true basketball genius—he is likely to be anointed by the wise men of hoops as a future prospect.

Brian Bowen Jr. never presented as the next LeBron James—that's a much smaller subset—but it was apparent from even before he hit his teens that he was a college prospect and possible NBA player. Both of his parents are over six feet tall. His extended family includes not just Jason Richardson, but others who had been top high school and college athletes. His own memory is that he never struggled or experienced a time when his coordination was still catching up with his height. When he played locally, he was always the best player on the court, bigger and faster than whatever competition he faced, and he could easily weave his way past defenders on the dribble or just shoot over them. He scored 48 points in his first game in middle school.

His game was a bit old school. He modeled it after Tracy McGrady, whose NBA career peaked before Tugs hit his teens, but he watched and rewatched the old tapes. Tugs admired McGrady's smoothness, the way he effortlessly changed speeds, how he blew by his defenders or just glided by. He liked Carmelo Anthony, a current NBA player, for the same reasons. It was a style thing. His favorite subject in school was history, and McGrady and Anthony would have been at home in the league a couple of decades earlier, in the era of short shorts and big Afros.

The summer after eighth grade, Bowen was invited to the CP3 Rising Stars Camp, named after the NBA star Chris Paul, and one of the stops on the circuit where a young player can make a name. "I was starting to blow up at that point," he said, "and then I played well there and it started to get really crazy."

When Tugs traveled outside of Saginaw, he got a sense of his growing profile. People knew his name. There were men watching from the sidelines he didn't know who came specifically to check him out. "You carry yourself different after you get known, hold your head a little higher," he said. "People are looking at you, there's expectations for you."

From middle school on, his peer group became the players he met at national events, others in the high school class of 2017 who projected as top recruits and future NBA first-round picks—including DeAndre Ayton, who would end up at Arizona; Marvin Bagley III, a Duke recruit; and Collin Sexton, who chose Auburn. They were all projected as one-and-done players, almost sure to bolt for the NBA after a single college season. Most evaluators did not put Tugs quite in their class, but that's who he measured himself against.

Bowen cracked the starting lineup at Arthur Hill High School in Saginaw as a freshman, which no one had done for years, and attracted intense attention from college coaches and the media. He played for a time for a local AAU program, Dorian's Pride, which was headed by the aspiring basketball impresario Christian Dawkins, and later played for a more prominent team in Chicago called MeanStreets. A story from when Bowen was fifteen described him as "a long lean guard with the ability to play nearly any position on the court," and it noted that through his cousin, Jason Richardson, he had already met LeBron James, Dwyane Wade, and other NBA stars.

After his sophomore season, Bowen left Saginaw and enrolled at La Lumiere prep in La Porte, Indiana. Michigan's state high school athletic board has some of the most restrictive rules in the country concerning where and when players can compete, and he wanted to be able to play in the made-for-TV games that ESPN and other commercial interests staged between the best high school teams. La Lumiere was a national power, but not what is sometimes referred to as a basketball factory, or a "pop-up basketball school"—schools created for basketball that sometimes do not even hold classes. (They outsource their academics to some nearby institution, or have their students take classes online.) Among La Lumiere's alumni is John Roberts, the chief justice of the Supreme Court.

Several of Bowen's teammates at La Lumiere were the targets of top Division I programs, including a player from Australia now playing at Creighton and another at Michigan State, Jaren Jackson Jr., who in 2018 would become a first-round NBA pick. Bowen figured he had the best of both worlds. "It's a legit school, but I was practicing every day against lottery picks."

If Bowen (or his father) were looking to increase his national profile and make himself an even hotter basketball stock, his transfer to La Lumiere accomplished that. But so did a couple of his other moves along the way. One was making it clear that despite his cousin's legacy at Michigan State, and the fact that he had a long-standing scholarship offer from coach Tom Izzo, the Spartans did not have an inside track. "It's nothing like that at all," he said when a reporter from the *Detroit Free Press* suggested it was a foregone conclusion that he would follow Jason Richardson's trail to East Lansing. He noted that the Spartans had been chasing him since "I was as small as I can be," but he was still shopping. He seemed to enjoy narrating the story of his recruitment.

In his junior year, he hinted that Michigan, in Ann Arbor— Michigan State and Tom Izzo's in-state rival—was a possibility even though they had not yet offered him a scholarship. "The relationship is getting pretty close," he said, sounding as if he were talking about his dating life. "Coach (John) Beilein likes to let his guards go. I've noticed that. I like to get up and down the floor really fast. That's a high-paced team. I'm interested."

Just after Christmas 2016, in an interview on Zagsblog (a recruiting site run by Adam Zagoria), he broke down the attributes of the five final schools on his list and how they were courting him. Arizona: "Big-time program. Their pitch is their style of play and the amount of guys they've got to the NBA at my position, so I really like that about them." Michigan State: "Has been on me for a good portion of my life." N.C. State: "They've been on me since ninth grade. They had a whole book of a plan for me. It means a lot." Creighton: "They've made a big leap in their program, and they want me to come in and make a bigger impact." Texas: "I know a couple guys down there, teammates I've played with. Coach (Shaka) Smart is a great guy, a great coach overall. Their pitch is that they really need a scorer, and I can bring that for them."

Like every player of his stature, Tugs was almost solely focused on what college program would best showcase him to the NBA and prepare him for pro success. He made the whole thing sound so wide open that many other programs, or at least their fan bases, seemed to feel they had a shot. A website called Addicted to Quack (it assiduously follows the Oregon Ducks) reported that Bowen might be headed to play basketball at Oregon. He seemed at times to be almost teasing Michigan State. "They're just saying I'm the No. 1, 2, and 3 plan," he said of Izzo and the Michigan State coaching staff. "I'm just the main guy that they really need or really want for next year." He was well known in the state, and when he attended Spartans games in East Lansing the crowd chanted his name, hoping to influence his decision.

Top high school players sometimes verbally commit in their junior year, or occasionally even earlier, though they can't formally sign scholarship offers until November of their senior year. It's not uncommon for them to back out of verbal commitments to "mid-majors," schools outside the premier conferences, if an offer from a more elite program comes along. (It's an axiom of the recruiting game that kids don't get recruited by the top schools until they have verbally committed somewhere else.)

But by the spring of any given year, most of the best players are formally signed. Bowen kept extending the process. The more players who committed, the more interest there was in him. He indicated he would make a decision by the end of January 2017, either in a press conference to be televised by ESPN or in a special video for the website Bleacher Report. "They've hit me up about it," he said, but there was no announcement and he remained on the market.

College recruiting for football and basketball is avidly followed, and there is money to be made from all the suspense and hype that swirls around questions over where seventeen- and eighteen-year-old athletes will choose to enroll. It is an obsession that has become an industry—and one of the countless ways in which profits are mined from young athletes. In this realm, no news or rumor is too small to publish or tweet.

Evan Daniels, one of the country's leading recruiting experts, sends out a blizzard of updates almost every day. A typical one: "Maros Zeliznak, a 6-11 center from Slovakia, just verbally committed to Jacksonville State, per a source." By interviewing kids after they make their recruiting visits ("Five-star forward E. J. Montgomery recaps official visit to Duke"), Daniels serves as an information clearinghouse for college coaches, who, even as they sometimes scoff at the veracity of the information on the recruiting sites, use them as a source of information on where their targets have visited and what they may be thinking.

In the last decade, the recruiting sites Scout.com and Rivals .com, along with SB Nation and 247Sports, which also focus heavily on recruiting, have been acquired by or merged with larger corporate partners in deals worth at least $300 million in total. Other sites, like MaxPreps, which covers high school sports in addition to just recruiting, have also been folded into bigger media companies. ESPN's massive TV and Internet empire exhaustively covers recruiting. All the major conferences operate websites, which drive traffic and earn advertising dollars by fixating on recruiting. There are some within this business who earn money as pseudo-journalists, reporting for the websites, and also double dip by selling their scouting information directly to college coaches. (The coaches, of course, expense it to their athletic departments.)

When Rivals was bought by Yahoo, a sports business columnist for CNBC wrote, "There is absolutely no slowdown in the interest of college/high school recruiting. The bottom line is that fans—especially in hard-core areas—can no longer afford to not know about the latest and greatest prospects their schools are recruiting. If they don't know the recruiting game, they'll lose at the water cooler. On National Football Signing Day, Rivals had 74 million page views."

By delaying his decision, Brian Bowen was serving an important service to this industry: He was providing content. What he did was more closely watched because he was still at large.

In the big grassroots youth basketball events, the results of the games matter less than the matchups of individual prospects, which play out as duels between high-end players trying to improve or justify their rankings. It is the major reason that the quality of play is generally considered wretched on the AAU circuit—and why many of the best high school players enter college with little idea how to play team basketball.

Bowen had solidified his stature while playing for the Chicago AAU club MeanStreets in a 2016 matchup against a team called Southern Stampede, which featured Collin Sexton, a speedy guard from suburban Atlanta who was already being projected as a possible NBA lottery pick. Sexton was four inches shorter and much quicker, and the two played different positions, but they guarded each other as dozens of college coaches watched from the bleachers. Sexton scored 33 points, but Bowen, with 19 points and seven rebounds, held his own and showed himself to be more than just a shooter. The game proved that he was a competent playmaker who could compete against a much quicker perimeter player, and it elevated his status.

In April 2017, Tugs traveled to New York to play in the annual Jordan Brand Classic, one of the highlights of the high school all-star basketball circuit. Past MVPs of the game, which would be televised by ESPN, included NBA superstars LeBron James, Kevin Durant, Kyrie Irving, and Anthony Davis. Like so much else about high school basketball, the event was half about the sport and half about the shoes.

During the week preceding the game, its sponsors staged a "Jordan Brand Classic Senior Night Tour," which consisted of visits to the schools of each participating player so a banner with their name and the name of the event could be hoisted in the gymnasium. La Lumiere got two banners—Bowen's, and one for his teammate and fellow Jordan Brand all-star Jaren Jackson Jr. Like many of the other institutions that supplied players to the Jordan Classic, La Lumiere was the type of school likely to attract future college players and NBA prospects. Whenever they walked into their practice gym, they would see the Jordan Brand banner.

Only a handful of the twenty-four participants were not yet committed to college programs, and they got special attention from the recruiting websites during the practice sessions leading up to the game. The players were also being watched by pro scouts, and by representatives of "mock draft" websites who predict the order of future drafts. "Brian Bowen has been great all week," Mike Schmitz of DraftExpress tweeted in the leadup to the game. "Shooting it in a variety of ways—spot-ups, off screens, one dribble pull-ups. Instinctual scorer."

His outstanding practice performances were prelude to a great game. Tugs connected on 10 of his 13 shots, including 6 of 7 of his three-point attempts, scored 26 points, and was named most valuable player of the East squad. Eric Bossi, a national basketball analyst for Rivals.com, noted the auspicious timing of Bowen's breakout performance. "Brian Bowen having himself by far the best day I've seen from him at any of the various all-star game circuit activities," he wrote, adding, "Picked a good time." A writer for Bleacher Report wrote that the "future of college basketball was on display" at Barclays Center—he was referring to all the players—but he singled out Bowen as particularly "poised and confident."

The site FanRag headlined a post in late May: "Where will Brian Bowen—the last uncommitted 5-star recruit—land?" It pointed out that he was the last of the top twenty recruits left and that there was only one other uncommitted prospect among the top hundred. "So what's the holdup for Tugs?" the story asked. "Simply put, no one knows." It listed five possible landing spots—none of them Louisville—and threw in Texas as a long shot because he had lately been retweeting a lot of Longhorn players.

One of the tropes of writing about college recruiting is for journalists to play the role of matchmakers. They look at the current roster of college teams, and perhaps the personality of the coaches and their preferred playing styles, and then opine on which players fit where. After watching him light up the scoreboard in Brooklyn, *Sports Illustrated*'s Luke Winn wrote of Bowen that he "could see why he'd be a great fit at Creighton." Exactly *why* he belonged at a Jesuit school in Omaha, Nebraska, that rarely advances very far into the NCAA tournament—and in some years does not even make the field—was not explained.

CHAPTER FOUR

THE 'VILLE

On July 28, 2010, Rick Pitino was called to the witness stand in a criminal trial at the federal courthouse in downtown Louisville. He was not the defendant, but his central role in the tawdry case was humiliating to him. Pitino was just about a decade into his stay in the city, and beloved. The wisecracking, Armani-dressed coach brought a taste of New York to Louisville, a sense that it was more than just a midsized city in Kentucky separated from Indiana by the Ohio River, and his games at the gleaming Yum Center, with its bourbon bars and luxury boxes, were as much about glitz as basketball.

Louisville is bigger in population than several cities with NBA teams, and there had long been a hope in town that it could attract a franchise. With Pitino, that desire became less urgent. "They were our pro team," Jonathan Blue, a former university trustee said. "The Yum Center was an NBA-like experience."

The defendant in the trial was Karen Cunagin Sypher, a blond former model. She was charged with trying to extort cash, cars, and a house from Pitino after they had sex in a restaurant banquette after closing time. He was the victim—and the star prosecution witness.

Pitino took the stand in a slim-fitting dark blue suit, white shirt, and red tie. He was without his usual pocket square. His wife, Joanne, was not in the courtroom. As he began his testimony, the prosecutor, assistant U.S. attorney Marisa Ford, asked him to state his profession, and after that formality, invited him to brag a little. It was her way of lifting him back onto his pedestal even as he sat in the witness box. "And you have met with a fair amount of success as a basketball coach, is that correct? . . . We may have members of the jury who are not basketball fans."

Pitino responded, "Well, the greatest thing about college basketball is you all start with the same dream. You all start, whether you're ranked No. 1 or ranked No. 300, you all have the same dream—that's to make the NCAA tournament at the end of the year. . . . It's called March Madness. It's what we all dream about and look forward to."

He explained how the tournament works—sixty-eight teams, a series of single-elimination games, all culminating on the third weekend with just four survivors.

"You've been to the Final Four?"

"Five times," Pitino answered.

Louisville is a notably gracious place, a smallish big city—population 616,000, twenty-ninth largest in the nation—that cherishes its traditions without seeming hidebound. Many of the buildings downtown still bear the engraved markings of what they once were: foundries, tobacco warehouses, confectioners, feed stores, pharmacies, and other long-gone establishments. The economy is driven now by Louisville-based Humana and other health care companies, two Ford plants on the city's periphery, a big United Parcel Service hub at the airport, Yum! Brands' (KFC, Taco Bell, and Pizza Hut) corporate headquarters, and a tourist industry invigorated by a new interest in bourbon. The Kentucky Derby at Churchill Downs is not just an event in May but a season unto itself, and not long after New Year's, a certain set of Louisville women begins shopping for dresses and hats. (The months before the Derby are also said to be high season for plastic surgery and Botox.)

There is an informal Catholic elite in Louisville, of which many of the men attended St. Xavier High School, known as "St. X."; a Protestant old-money crowd that gathers at the exclusive Louisville Country Club; and a not insubstantial Jewish population with roots in bourbon and retail.

The city has a complicated racial history. It was one of the nation's largest slave-trading hubs, and Kentucky was a so-called slave-growing state, where children born into slavery were sold to planters in the Deep South. By many historical accounts, Louisville is where the phrase "sold down the river"—it refers to slaves being auctioned and sent down the Ohio to where it meets the Mississippi near Cairo, Illinois, and then on south toward New Orleans—originated.

Kentucky, however, declared itself neutral at the beginning of the Civil War and Louisville itself was a Union stronghold. In the years that followed, the city was more racially progressive than the rest of Kentucky and—in relative terms only—more benign than much of the South. Long before Jim Crow laws were overturned elsewhere, black residents of Louisville could shop in downtown department stores. (They were not allowed to try on clothes.) The streetcars were integrated from early in the twentieth century. Louisville's mayors and other power brokers have tended to be white liberals. Muhammad Ali, born Cassius Clay in one of the city's historically black neighborhoods, kept a residence in Louisville until his death and remains a great point of pride for the city.

The University of Louisville has long been an essential part of the city's fabric. It began as a struggling seminary in 1798 and later added a medical school and law school, which also struggled. Early in the twentieth century, it became more of a complete university, adding courses of study in the sciences and liberal arts, but until 1970 it remained a "municipal" institution rather than part of Kentucky's higher education system. Because it was not a state school, segregation laws did not apply in the same way, and the U. of L. integrated before the state's flagship university in Lexington, as did its basketball team.

Under longtime coach Bernard Hickman, Louisville brought on its first black players in 1962, a decade before Adolph Rupp, Kentucky's legendary coach, recruited his first (and only) black player. A couple of years later, Louisville landed prized recruit Wes Unseld, whose family members were pillars of the city's African American community going back several generations. Unseld's late brother, George, became a longtime city councilman, and there is an Unseld Boulevard in Louisville.

The university's mission was to educate the working-class daughters and sons of Louisville, white and black, and if the campus was ugly and unalluring it didn't matter as much because few of its students could afford room and board. They lived at home and fit their studies around the jobs they worked to pay their tuition.

The term "commuter school" is often used as a pejorative, with little regard for the importance that such institutions have played in Louisville and other American cities. When these schools transform themselves and "elevate" the quality of their incoming students while adding campus amenities—well-appointed dormitories with suites and kitchens; workout facilities for students that are the equivalent of high-end health clubs; dining facilities with vegan and gluten-free menus—and after tuitions go up commensurately, it is never clear what happens to the students these institutions *used* to serve. That, however, became the new goal at Louisville—to move on from its past and become a reborn institution, one that was recognized nationally.

Pitino lent the U. of L. his style and swagger, and those qualities conveyed to greater Louisville. Tom Jurich, as he did with every asset he assembled, maximized Pitino's impact. He multiplied it. The new stadiums and arenas, the wealthy donors who put up the money, the national profile of U. of L. sports, the unassailable status of the athletic department within the university—all of it was built on Pitino's celebrity and Jurich's smarts.

Jurich reaped the benefits of Pitino's coaching genius and magnetic personality. In return, the coach got everything he wanted: The resources he needed to build a team. The big salary. And the benefit of the doubt, always. When Pitino stepped out of line, or when his program fell into disgrace, Jurich turned a blind eye. The whole city did.

Jurich and the university's entrepreneurial president through most of his tenure, James Ramsey, revolutionized the U. of L. A depressing campus became much more attractive, even lively, especially after dark, when it used to be deserted. Louisville became a destination that students *chose,* rather than one that was their only option.

Jerry Abramson served five terms as Louisville's mayor between 1986 and 2011 and was involved in nearly every aspect of the changes the university brought to south Louisville. "Ramsey got the private sector to build dorms," he said. "Freshmen had to live on campus. He wanted commercial activity—restaurants and retail and bars—and all that came to fruition. He also attracted an entering freshman class with higher ACT and SAT scores. For the first nine or ten years, he was a superstar. He did it all right."

The university attained more of a national reputation, and, perhaps even more remarkably, it became an emblem of civic pride, even among well-heeled Louisvillians. They still may not have wanted to send their kids there—academic standards never did rise to any great heights—but they became dues-paying members of Cardinal Nation.

It is hard to overstate the power Jurich had in Louisville—he was on any short list of its most powerful citizens, just a notch below Senate majority leader Mitch McConnell. It is wrong to think he was involved in a cynical pursuit at Louisville. Jurich was a true believer in the centrality of sports at the U. of L., or on any college campus. His job, as he understood it, was to bring excitement and a sense of unity to campus, raise increasingly large sums of money, and expand the physical and psychic footprint of sports. All good things would come from that. He didn't question it.

The Jurichs raised their children in Louisville; all four graduated from the university, and three were varsity athletes. After he was dismissed, Tom and Terrilynn Jurich retreated with their chocolate Lab to their lakeside home in Steamboat Springs, Colorado, at the base of 6,900-foot Mount Werner. The fastidiously restored downtown—a few blocks of brick storefronts, brewhouses, and bistros—was about a mile away. Jurich, sixty-one, was on the slopes every other day, which was as much as his knees would permit, and Terrilynn, the former Miss Wyoming, threw herself into cross-country skiing.

At dinner one night at a restaurant in town, they clasped hands and said grace. Tom Jurich had a couple of beers, his wife a glass of red wine. "I'm sorry," Terrilynn said at one point during dinner as she cried softly. "We really haven't talked to anybody about this. But Louisville was our home. It's where our family grew up together and it was very painful to have to leave."

Being an athletic director is not a job that many people aspire to from a young age. It wouldn't make sense. There are fewer than four hundred of them at the Division I level, and far fewer at the top tier. Tom Jurich was a multisport high school athlete, a college football player, and then very briefly a placekicker in the NFL. He played one game for the New Orleans Saints in 1978, missed all three of his field goal tries (two of them from close range), and was immediately released, never to play in the league again.

Jurich was raised in Southern California, but after his exit from the NFL, he returned to Flagstaff, Arizona, where he had played football at Northern Arizona. He sold real estate and dabbled in a couple of other business ventures while helping out his alma mater with fund-raising. At twenty-nine years old, and much to his surprise, he was offered a job as the university's athletic director. "There was no such thing as a revenue sport there," he said. The basketball team drew crowds of about 6,000; the football team sometimes filled its 15,000-seat stadium. (The football program, however, was an incubator for future NFL coaches—Andy Reid, Brad Childress, and Marty Mornhinweg passed through Northern Arizona during Jurich's time.)

After eight years, Jurich left Flagstaff to become athletic director at Colorado State. The job was a step up, and its location, in Fort Collins, was not far from Terrilynn's parents in Wyoming. In 1997, when Louisville approached him, he had no intention at first of even listening. He had never lived east of Colorado. He had been to Ohio a few times to visit relatives, and to New York just once. The job itself was unalluring in the extreme. "The athletic facilities were horrific," he said. "It was a commuter school and virtually no one lived on campus. The football team had just gone 1–10. The basketball team was 12–20. Women's sports didn't exist. We had a swim team, but we barely had chlorine to put in the pool. It was all bad. Every friend I had in the business said I was making a mistake. They perceived it as a step down, and to be honest, I had turned down better jobs."

But Louisville was persistent. They offered a long-term deal (because of state law in Colorado, Jurich was working a contract that had to be renewed annually) that would just about double his salary. The Jurichs had a young family and it seemed irresponsible not to listen. (Their two sons were Jurich's from a first marriage, but he had custody from the time they were young.) Once he relented and agreed that they would visit the campus, he and his wife had already decided he would accept the job.

Louisville at the time was under threat of being kicked out of Conference USA, a mix of geographically and culturally misaligned public and private institutions that included Cincinnati, Marquette, Tulane, Southern Mississippi, Houston, South Florida, and DePaul.

Its failure to comply with Title IX gender equity standards was an issue, low attendance was a problem, and nothing about Louisville's sports program added luster to the conference. Jurich's credibility, more than any other factor, kept them from being ousted. Athletic directors at the other schools in the conference believed him when he said he could set Louisville on a better course.

College coaches preach to their teams about the value of loyalty and steadfastness, but at the upper levels of the NCAA, universities run from conference to conference, chasing richer TV deals. It's a game of mergers and acquisitions—of running out on your partners before they run out on you—and Jurich knew how to play it. He got Louisville into the old Big East Conference, "and that was a magical spot for us," he said, because the conference was largely an assemblage of other city schools, including Georgetown, Pitt, and Cincinnati. But the Big East splintered, and he needed to look elsewhere. The Cardinals moved to the American Athletic Conference but stayed for just one year. When Maryland, a member of the Atlantic Coast Conference, bolted for the Big Ten, Jurich saw an opening. "That's when I pounced," he said.

"Most people would say the greatest moment in Louisville sports history was getting into the ACC, but that's not what I think," Jurich said. "It was the day we didn't get kicked out of Conference USA. Where were we going to go from there? You have nowhere to go. You're done."

Above all, Jurich understood college sports as entertainment. To resurrect Louisville's moribund football program, he brought in an offensive-minded coach named John L. Smith, whose motto was "first team to 50 wins." But when Smith said he would win the conference within three years, even Jurich didn't believe him. His response, as he recalls it, was, "Are you on drugs?"

In Smith's first year, the team suffered two bad losses to open the season, and then went on the road to play Illinois—not a good team, but still a member of the powerful Big Ten Conference. The Cardinals won in a romp, 35–9, which Jurich considered "the most shocking thing I've ever seen." From a one-victory season the previous year, Louisville went on to finish with a 7–5 record and a bowl game appearance. That it was just the Motor City Bowl in Detroit did not make it any less miraculous. In three separate games, the Cardinals scored more than 60 points. The last home game of the previous season had drawn an announced crowd of 12,850 (people who were there said it was less); John L. Smith's "basketball on grass" style attracted crowds of 40,000-plus. An expansion of the football stadium, already under way when Jurich arrived, suddenly made sense.

Even revived, Louisville football was hardly on a par with Notre Dame, Michigan, or other traditional powers, and it was not going to get any of the prominent time slots on the weekend schedule of televised football. Jurich figured out a solution. "Louisville came to us and said, 'We'll play anyone, anywhere, anytime,'" Mark Shapiro, a former head of programming and production at ESPN, told the *New York Times* in 2013. The Cardinals became a staple on Tuesday nights, an otherwise slack time in sports programming. "It was a programmer's dream," Shapiro said. "We already had NFL on Sunday nights, NHL and MLB on multiple nights, Thursday night college football. We were all filled up. So I said, 'How about Tuesday nights?' They seized it, and over time their results have been spectacular."

Louisville's midweek slot on ESPN also served as a recruiting tool. The top high school prospects want to be on TV and will not even consider a program that is not regularly featured on national broadcasts. Stefan LeFors, a high school player in Louisiana, had no interest in Louisville and only a passing familiarity with them until he watched them win an exciting overtime game against Army. "That was the only reason Louisville was on my list," he said. He reached out to the coaches and ended up as a two-year starter at quarterback.

Jurich's next task was to fix the basketball program, which was in some ways more difficult—and certainly more delicate. Unlike football, basketball at Louisville had a rich tradition, but it was embodied by a coach who was still on the scene: Denny Crum, a former assistant to John Wooden at UCLA who led the Cardinals to national championships in 1980 and 1986. Crum was entering his twenty-seventh season when Jurich arrived in 1997, and his program was stagnant at best; it made the NCAA tournament most years but rarely advanced far. In the 2000–2001 season, the team bottomed out with a 12–19 record, and many of the losses, including a 34-point blowout at home to Charlotte, were not even close.

Jurich decided he needed to replace Crum, who had 675 career victories, but the two engaged in a weeks-long standoff, a "battle of wills," as one account called it at the time, as the coach resisted stepping down and Jurich hesitated to fire him. Crum finally retired, accepting a $2 million buyout and $5 million to work as a university consultant over the next fifteen years. (That figure would go up considerably over time, as did just about every other athletic department salary and expense.)

In selecting a new basketball coach, Jurich focused, as always, on generating buzz and big money. The hiring of Smith to coach football was a step in the right direction, but the athletic department's finances were still dire. "With Coach Crum, I thought we were going south," he said. "We had to make a change, but I had to think big, and I felt like I wanted to replace a Hall of Fame coach with a Hall of Fame coach. In our blue state," he continued—blue being a reference not to politics, but to the state's majority preference for University of Kentucky basketball—"Rick Pitino was Elvis. I thought with him, we could sell out our fan base."

In particular, Jurich needed to win back longtime season-ticket holders who had dropped away and well-heeled donors who were no longer giving. At the time, there did not seem to be any ethical concerns about Pitino other than a little-remembered report involving NCAA violations going back to his time at Hawaii in the mid-1970s. The NCAA found that Pitino had provided round-trip airfare for a player between New York and Honolulu, arranged for some players to receive cars in exchange for season tickets, and gave out coupons for free food at McDonald's. (The last benefit, free McDonald's food, is almost a parody of the picayune violations that NCAA critics find so objectionable.)

But the NCAA also found that Pitino and the head coach at the time, Bruce O'Neill, provided false information to investigators and ordered the two men to be disassociated from the program, at a point after they had already left. The *New York Times* unearthed details of the episode when Pitino was under consideration for the Kentucky head coaching job in 1989. He could have responded that he had made mistakes as a young coach years back, but, typically, he insisted that he had done nothing wrong. "There's no one in this business with more integrity than Rick Pitino," he said. "I'm going to make my mistakes as a coach—every coach is going to make mistakes. But one thing you won't have to worry about is cheating with Rick Pitino. It didn't happen in Hawaii as far as I'm concerned."

When the reporter followed up, Pitino held firm. "I was a graduate assistant. I didn't make any mistakes, I don't care what anybody says."

The incident did not deter Kentucky, and by the time Louisville began recruiting him, it was twenty-five years in the past. Common friends in Louisville connected Jurich with Pitino, who was temporarily out of a job, having resigned as the coach of the Boston Celtics the previous season. Pitino was not one to want to sit around, but when Jurich flew down to Miami to meet with him in the spring of 2001, he was no more eager to come to Louisville than Jurich had been a few years earlier. "I made my pitch, but he rejected me," Jurich said. "It went on for three weeks and he rejected me three different times."

Pitino thought the fans at Kentucky would hate him and those at Louisville, his former rival, would never embrace him. (He was right on the first count.) He couldn't wrap his mind around returning to college coaching ninety miles from Lexington. But he considered himself a turnaround artist, like a CEO who revives failing companies, and Jurich persuaded him to view the Louisville job that way. "My vision to him was we can turn this thing around." Jurich also sensed, correctly, that after life in the NBA cities of New York and Boston, Joanne Pitino was eager to return to quieter surroundings.

Rick Pitino would come to feel the same way. Louisville suited him. "It's the finest place I've lived, because it incorporates everything that I want in my life," he said in 2013. "I like good restaurants. I like the Thoroughbred industry. I like very little traffic because I grew up with traffic. So it offers me everything that I want in my life, and then, if I want an amenity, I go to New York or I go to Miami, where I have residences."

In their sixteen years together, Pitino and Jurich were business associates but never friends. Jurich grew up almost within sight of the Santa Anita racetrack in Arcadia, California (his high school shared a parking lot with it), so a love of Thoroughbred racing was one thing they did share. But Jurich could not remember them ever having dinner alone. "He had his own set of friends," he said. "I stay with my wife and family."

The Pitino who was a creature of the night was no secret in Louisville, but Jurich says he had no direct knowledge and not much interest in that aspect of his coach. "People see Rick as the guy in Armani suits. I saw him as a different person. To me, he was the guy in a sweatsuit, in the gym with his players."

Jurich's father was an executive with Transamerica, and he drilled into him that an effective leader hires good people and supports them. "I have been criticized for being too loyal," he said, "but I can't be disloyal. It's not in my DNA."

The episode at the heart of the Karen Sypher affair occurred seven years before the trial, in 2003, at a favorite haunt of Pitino's, an Italian restaurant called Porcini a couple of miles from his home. He had just hired a new assistant coach, former NBA player Reggie Theus, and to celebrate he put together a golf outing with Theus and a couple of friends. They played at a local country club in the afternoon, agreeing that the losers would buy dinner, and then met that evening at the restaurant.

Pitino had what he described as a designated driver with him, a noncoaching member of his basketball staff, and the table drank several bottles of wine. According to his testimony, when dinner was over he moved to the corner of the bar to talk with some friends. Karen Sypher, who was then forty-three years old, approached. (Her last name then was her maiden name, Cunagin.) Pitino, then fifty, had never met her before. She asked if he could wish her son a happy birthday, which he did, adding, "Study hard in school."

The restaurant was clearing out and Pitino believed Sypher had left, but she came back later and edged next to him at the bar. She told him she was a big Louisville basketball fan. He was drinking a glass of wine. "I ordered a drink for her and she started rubbing on my leg," he testified.

As this was going on, his friends melted away, leaving him with a woman he had just met. It seemed like the kind of moment where they may have had an idea of what might, or would, happen next. They were giving Coach Pitino his space.

When the last of the other patrons had left, the owner of the restaurant walked over and said, "Coach, I'm going to head home. You'll finish your drink and leave?" Pitino said that would be fine, and the owner said, "Okay, go out the side door," indicating that it would lock behind him.

According to Pitino's testimony, after they found themselves alone, Sypher said to him, "Why don't we finish our drinks over there?" as she looked in the direction of a banquette. "We did and then some unfortunate things happened."

He said he had too much to drink to drive but was otherwise "totally coherent."

"Did you have sex?" the prosecutor asked.

"Yes, very briefly."

The details of the case were sordid almost beyond words. It reflected poorly on Pitino, but on the other hand, his response to the attempted extortion showed his competitive instincts. As mortifying as it all was, he was determined not to lose. Someone had tried to get the best of him, and rather than surrender to it, he went to law enforcement.

On the witness stand, he explained why the sexual encounter was so brief. "She opened my pants and asked if I had a condom and I said no, I don't carry condoms with me." She joked that she was very fertile, to the point that when her ex-husband even just looked at her, she got pregnant. "And I got very scared at that point," Pitino testified. "Our encounter lasted less than fifteen seconds. . . . We talked a little bit. I pulled my pants up and we left a short time afterwards."

Under cross-examination by Sypher's lawyer, James Earhart, he was pressed for more detail. "I immediately pulled out," Pitino said.

"You did not ejaculate, then?" the lawyer asked him.

"I did," he said. "Down my leg."

Beyond the incident itself, the trial revealed something about the world Pitino inhabited, and it provided a window into his day-to-day life. He was a wealthy, powerful, and busy man, and he had people around him who saw to his needs and, when necessary, carried out some difficult tasks.

About three weeks after their encounter, he testified that he got a call from Sypher, who told him she had missed her period. He said he did not think the baby could possibly be his, but when she asked for $3,000, he provided it. He then arranged for an employee of Louisville basketball, his equipment manager, to drive her to Cincinnati, where she got an abortion. In court, Pitino insisted he believed the $3,000 was to pay for her health insurance and not specifically for an abortion.

Pitino's equipment manager was Tim Sypher. He had worked for Pitino going back to when he was coaching the Boston Celtics. His role was what in politics is called a "body man." He spent time with Pitino, drove him, ran errands, took care of business. Tim Sypher got to know the former Karen Cunagin on the drive to Cincinnati and back. They began dating. Eventually they married, and she became Karen Sypher. (The two gave new meaning to the phrase "meet cute.")

It was not until six years later that Pitino began getting threatening messages on his cell phone. A male voice alleged that Pitino had raped Karen Sypher and said that the allegation, if made public, would harm his public image. (The Syphers were having marital problems and the voice on the messages was not Tim Sypher's, but a male associate of Karen Sypher's, according to testimony at the trial.)

Pitino suspected that Karen Sypher was behind the threats, and said to her husband, "You need to get your wife and we need to talk." They met soon after that, and a few days later, according to the criminal complaint, Pitino received the first of a series of written messages from her, demanding college tuition for her children, two cars, a paid-off house, and $3,000 a month. She wrote, "If all is accepted, I will protect Rick Pitino's name for life." An attorney working for Sypher later elevated the demand to $10 million.

Sypher's son, then twenty, was one of the people who attempted to negotiate a settlement from Pitino. When he raised the rape allegation, Pitino testified, he told him, "I can assure you, son, that never happened."

On cross-examination, Sypher's lawyer questioned why Pitino did not immediately call law enforcement rather than try to deal with it himself, which he did for about a month. It was a season in which his team fell just one game short of advancing to the Final Four, and the phone messages and demands had started in late February, on the eve of the annual event he had told the jury about— March Madness. "I don't think you understand what was going on in my life at that point," he answered. "We were trying to win a championship, and I was trying to coach this team to a championship."

Pitino's back-and-forth with Sypher's lawyer was contentious. "No, I did not pay for the abortion," he testified, adding that he did not believe the procedure cost $3,000.

"We're going to banter over this?" Earhart said.

"We are," Pitino replied.

He testified that he had "deep regret" for embarrassing and humiliating the university and his family. "Ignorance on my part led up to it," he said. "I'm a married man and I never should have put myself in that situation."

Pitino was known for his pithy press conferences, and some fans looked forward to his postgame badinage with the media almost as much as the games themselves. Once, as he was talking, a smartphone that had been placed on the podium by a reporter to record him began to ring. He picked it up. "Hello?" he said. "Yes . . . Where do you want to meet for a drink? . . . Who's we?" He put it down and said, "Some people want to have a drink with you, Bob, and they said they want to meet at Jeff Ruby's." His press conference after the Sypher affair became public was uncharacteristically somber. After the news broke, he said, "I went home to comfort my wife because this has been pure hell for her." But he also took pains to assure the team's fans, known as Cardinal Nation, that the program would not be damaged. "We will continue to bring in great players," he said. "We will continue to run this program with great integrity."

Sypher was convicted and did serious prison time—six and a half years, some of it in an eight-by-ten-foot cell, with a roommate, at the Marianna prison camp in Florida. She was denied early release by Charles Simpson III, the federal judge who presided over her trial, and served her full term. When he sentenced her initially, Simpson, who got his undergraduate and law degrees at the University of Louisville, said Sypher's crimes were "brazen, driven by sheer greed and desire for money, and for a lifestyle which the defendant must have desired."

Jurich considered Pitino's lapse with Karen Sypher to be a private affair. And considering Pitino's income, he reasoned that he could have paid to silence her but did the right thing by going to law enforcement. (That may not be the case since her last demand was for $10 million.) "She was on a mission to get him," Jurich said after the trial. "It's been very taxing because he loves his family. He knows he let them down that night."

In one sense, Pitino prevailed. He did not cave to extortion, and Sypher paid a heavy price. But he suffered permanent damage. It was her trial, but it was *his* reputation and legacy at stake, and the image of a fifty-year-old man with his pants down in a restaurant booth is everlasting.

Around the time of the trial, Mike Lupica, the *New York Daily News* columnist, referred to the Sypher affair as a "shabby mess" and wrote, "It is why for all the games he has won at Louisville and will continue to win, Pitino is through there, sooner rather than later."

Pitino *was* through in one sense, in that the old image of Rick

Pitino—the mentor-coach, leader of young men, and inculcator of off-court values—was dead. That was a role for someone else to play. Pitino had lost his claim to it. But the university's leadership was not as bothered as Lupica seemed to imagine they would be. They were happy to keep him.

His mission was clarified after the Sypher affair. From that point on, it was only about winning games, generating revenue, and entertaining greater Louisville.

Those, of course, were Pitino's primary objectives from the start—and the same is true of every coach in every revenue-producing sport at every university in the nation that plays big-time sports. Win. Entertain. Put asses in the seats. Make money. Everything else is secondary. It's possible you'll get fired for something that happens on the periphery. The surer thing is that you won't stay in the job very long just for being a straitlaced Boy Scout if you can't compete at the top of the conference, fill the arena, and get into postseason play.

CHAPTER FIVE

ABSOLUTIONS

I t is easy to lose sight of what a genius of a coach Pitino has been. When a sports legacy is sullied, it has the effect of erasing memories and moments.

Pitino was a master of motivation, game preparation, and in-game tactics. If you asked anyone inside college basketball what coach they would choose to win just one game—not necessarily a program builder or leader of young men, but the guy to get a victory when it was most needed—Pitino would be at or near the top of any list. There's a quote attributed to the late football coach Bum Phillips about Alabama's legendary Paul Bryant—"He can take his'n and beat your'n, and then he can turn around and take your'n and beat his'n"—and you could say the same about Pitino. If the talent levels were equal, he was probably going to win.

Pitino's first Final Four team, Providence College in 1987,

established his bona fides because he had so little to work with. There are some 4,500 Division I basketball players at any given time, and Pitino's point guard, Billy Donovan, now the head coach of the NBA's Oklahoma City Thunder, would have been way down on the list of the ones you would want to build a Final Four team around. He was overweight and out of shape when Pitino arrived before his junior year. He had averaged less than three points a game over his first two seasons and wanted to transfer. Pitino called around to other coaches to try to find him a spot, and then had to inform Donovan that no one else wanted to offer him a scholarship, so he might as well stay.

But Pitino liked Donovan's skills and said that if he worked on his fitness, he could earn playing time. He also suggested he learn to take a jump shot. (Donovan had been getting just a couple of inches off the ground on his attempts—almost like he was taking an old-fashioned set shot.) "Coach was brutally honest, and Billy embraced his message," Herb Sendek, an assistant to Pitino at Providence, recalls. "There's never been a player before or since who transformed himself like Billy did."

In his first year with Pitino, the newly svelte Donovan played 30 minutes a game and averaged 15 points, and Providence won 17 games, a big improvement over the previous season but not enough to make the NCAA tournament. They did make it to the semifinals of the National Invitation Tournament.

The following season, 1986–87, was the first year of the three-point shot in college basketball. Most coaches scorned it as a gimmick and let their players attempt only a handful of them a game. Pitino embraced the new rule as an equalizer—a way for an undersized, moderately talented team to overachieve. In doing so, he established the model for the Cinderella Final Four teams that followed—from Butler to George Mason to Virginia Common-wealth—all of them with small but skilled players who spaced the floor and took copious numbers of three-point shots. Providence that season attempted nearly three times as many three-pointers as its opponents. Donovan alone launched seven a game, connecting on 40 percent of them.

Pitino figured out the geometry of the modern game before anyone else—space the floor with shooters—and its new math. A team that connected on even 35 percent of its three-point attempts was better off than one that traditionally "worked the ball in" closer to the hoop and took two-pointers, especially if those two-point attempts were closely guarded, or out near the new three-point line where you might as well take a step back beyond the arc and let it fly.

This was not the way that Pitino's teams always played in the years that followed—the team was uncharacteristically weak defensively—but it was the way that his Providence team needed to play. The Friars went on an astounding late-season charge before getting stopped one game short of the NCAA title game by Syracuse, led by future NBA all-star Derrick Coleman. It was Pitino's last game at Providence. Over the next two decades, he would bounce between the NBA and college basketball, from the Knicks, to Kentucky, and and on to the Celtics before landing at Louisville.

The Sypher trial took place nine years into Pitino's Louisville reign, after one Final Four and two Elite Eight appearances. After its conclusion, Pitino repaid Jurich's loyalty and the support of the university administration by doing what he does best: creating teams that amounted to more than the sum of their parts.

The season that immediately followed the trial was solid, 25 wins against 10 losses, but the Cardinals were knocked out of the NCAA tournament by a lower-seeded opponent, Morehead State, in a first-round upset. The next season Pitino's squad piled up 30 wins and reached the Final Four before losing to archrival Kentucky in the semifinal game.

What came next, in 2012–13, was quintessential Pitino. He had lightly recruited players and castoffs, most of them distinctly non-NBA prospects. Peyton Siva, his point guard, was an undersized kid from Seattle of Samoan descent. (He played 24 games for the Detroit Pistons before hooking on with the Fort Wayne Mad Ants of the NBA's development league, and then decamped for pro ball in Europe.) The other guard, Russ Smith, had such a penchant for attempting difficult plays and taking crazy shots that Pitino gave him the nickname "Russdiculous."

The roster included just one NBA first-round draft choice, Gorgui Dieng, a junior taken with the twenty-third pick, and a typical Pitino recruit: Coming out of high school, he picked Louisville over a small group of suitors that included Marquette and Marshall. He was a nice player, but the top teams were not knocking down his door. Pitino specialized in taking players like Dieng, "coaching them up," as it is said in the business, and blending them with their similarly good-but-not-great teammates. It was basketball as alchemy.

As motley as this Pitino team seemed to outsiders, it cohered from day one. The group played with such incredible togetherness and grit that they inspired devotion from those who understood the game. "The most inspirational team I've ever covered," veteran basketball writer Reid Forgrave observed in a piece for CBSSports.com.

Early in February, Notre Dame managed to defeat Louisville, 104–101, in South Bend—but it took five overtimes to finish them off. And it was the last game the Cardinals would lose.

Pitino's team entered the postseason as the top seed in the Midwest region and the overall No. 1 seed in the tournament. They cruised through the early rounds, routing North Carolina A&T and Colorado State, and then struggled to an 8-point victory over Oregon that felt even closer than the score indicated. "Russdiculous" Smith saved them by relentlessly driving to the hoop, and Oregon could only stop him by fouling. He scored 31 points, 12 of them on free throws.

Louisville qualified for the Final Four two days later with a 22-point victory over Duke, a game best remembered for a gruesome lower leg fracture suffered by one of Pitino's key subs, Kevin Ware. The game was close at halftime, with Louisville holding just a three-point lead, but their cloying defense and ferocious pursuit of loose balls and rebounds led to a 20–4 run early in the second half.

Afterward, Duke coach Mike Krzyzewski described the experience of playing a Pitino team. "I thought we had a chance there, and then, boom," he said. "That's what they do to teams. They can boom you." Oregon's coach, Dana Altman, made a similar comment after falling in the previous game. "They get on those runs, they just multiply points, they don't add them," he said.

Pitino coached by feel. Not all coaches can do that. It takes confidence and the ability (and credentials) to withstand second-guessing and criticism. In the national semifinal game against Wichita State, at the Georgia Dome in Atlanta, Louisville emerged with a four-point victory in large part because Pitino entrusted minutes to a couple of bench players who only occasionally got playing time at key moments.

Tim Henderson, who played high school ball at Christian Academy in Louisville, was a nonscholarship walk-on who had begged for a spot on the team by writing to Pitino—not by email, but actual letters with stamps on them. He connected on two three-point baskets in the semifinal game. Stephan Van Treese was a highly ranked prospect in his mid-teens but the top programs "all backed off," one recruiting site said, after he struggled against his peers on the summer AAU circuit. At Indiana, his home-state school, it was said that "the likelihood of a scholarship being extended is basically non-existent." He played ten productive minutes against Wichita and came up with three rebounds, a blocked shot, and a steal. (The six-foot-ten Van Treese would go on to have a pro career—in Japan with the Fukushima Firebonds, where he was known as the Vanilla Godzilla.) The big star of the Wichita game was a senior who came off the bench and scored 20 points, another unlikely hero—Luke Hancock, a transfer who had spent the first two years of his college career playing for George Mason.

The victory put Louisville into the championship game against Michigan, which had all the pedigree that Pitino's roster lacked. Two of its players, Glenn Robinson III and Tim Hardaway Jr., were the sons of former NBA players. Three of the Wolverines would be first-round picks, two of them lottery choices.

As the game started, Pitino took his usual pose on the sideline— standing, legs spread a little, knees bent, usually one shoe on the playing surface unless the action was right in front of him. He was a point guard at the University of Massachusetts, had never put on much weight, and never looked like he didn't still want to go out and guard somebody. He often clasped his hands behind his back, as if to prevent himself from reaching out for the ball.

Michigan got out to a big early lead largely because one of its own little-used players, Spike Albrecht (the name sounded like it was out of juvenile sports fiction), was experiencing some kind of out-of-body experience. He averaged 1.8 points a game for the season, but by the end of the first half he had 17 points—some of which came on closely guarded three-point shots that he put up when he barely had a view of the basket.

Pitino kept his jaw set and a couple of times a thin smile emerged. He had the look of a man who knew that he was not going to get beat by a fairy tale. Hancock, Louisville's hero from the semifinal game, hit a couple of outside shots, the defense clamped down on Albrecht, and at halftime, a 12-point Michigan lead had shrunk to one point.

Pitino had one more unorthodox move in him. Russ Smith had been his most indispensable player for most of the season and through the early games of the tournament. After his fierce effort in the Oregon game the previous weekend, Pitino said, "Without Russ Smith, we couldn't win."

But as the second half of the national championship game began, Smith was on the bench and Hancock, usually a substitute, was on the court. Very few coaches would do that, but Smith had not played well, and Pitino knew his team needed to start the half better than it began the game.

The best of Pitino's teams were miserable to play against. Against Michigan, they came out in the second half double-teaming the ball, switching, swarming, chesting up against ball handlers. For most of the last 20 minutes they maintained a small lead that somehow seemed bigger. Michigan struggled to advance the ball past half-court within the allowable 10 seconds, and they had to hit some very difficult shots just to keep the game close.

Russ Smith reentered and hit a big three-point shot. Then he drove to the basket and kicked it back to Hancock for a three-pointer. Few teams turn the screws like Pitino's. They went ferociously after their own missed shots and in the second half were plus-12 in rebounding. Louisville prevailed, 82–76. Pitino had his second national championship, the first having come back in 1996, at Kentucky. Hancock, who scored 22 points, was named the tournament's most outstanding player—the first substitute ever to win the award.

When Pitino returned home to Louisville after the championship, he fulfilled a promise he had made to his players—that he would get a tattoo if they won. He opted to have it drawn on his left shoulder blade. It was big and bold—the university's old-English "L" emblem in red, surrounded by the words "NCAA champions" and the season record, "35–5." In the days that followed, it seemed like just about everybody in Louisville viewed the YouTube video of a bare-chested Pitino getting inked. "It was the porn the whole town was watching," one longtime resident called it.

It was a glorious time for Pitino. A Thoroughbred he partly owned, Goldencents, won the Santa Anita Derby, qualifying it to run in the Kentucky Derby a few weeks after the national title game. Purchased at auction, the horse was described in one account as if it could have been a player on his team—"a relatively small bay colt with a modest pedigree."

Pitino's national title was just one chapter of a magical few months in Louisville sports—the fulfillment of Tom Jurich's vision, except that it was beyond even what he could have imagined. In January 2013, the football team pulled off a huge upset in the Sugar Bowl, defeating No. 4–ranked Florida, which was favored by two touchdowns. The women's basketball team made it all the way to the final game of the NCAA tournament before being defeated by Connecticut. (Jurich spent the weekend flying back and forth between the men's and women's games.) The baseball team advanced into the College World Series. Louisville became the first university with two Final Four teams, a winner in a BCS bowl game, and a participant in the College World Series in a single year.

To commemorate what became known as the Year of the Cardinal, the university splurged to have a video company produce a documentary and purchased one hour of airtime for it to run on ESPNU. "It was a year of excellence," the narrator intones at the beginning. "A destiny was realized. An impossible dream came true. . . . For the University of Louisville, it was a year like no other."

It was also the last great chapter of the Pitino era. In October 2015, a Louisville woman and self-described escort, Katina Powell, published a book in which she told of parties—inside the basketball dorm—where she provided women to dance for high school players being recruited by Pitino, and for some of his current players as well. She said she was paid for these services by Andre McGee, a former player for Pitino who was serving as his director of basketball operations. The dancers included Powell's two adult daughters.

The book was called *Breaking Cardinal Rules: Basketball and the Escort Queen* and written with journalist Dick Cady. "At the peak of the dormitory and off-campus entertainment more than $10,000 cash changed hands to Katina for supplying the women," it alleged. "This does not include the hundreds of one-dollar bills thrown at the dancers. . . . Nor does it include the money paid to the women who had sex with the recruits afterward. So frequent were the escapades that Katina would later say, especially after the Cardinals won the 2012–13 NCAA championship, 'I felt like I was part of the recruitment team. A lot of them players went to Louisville because of me.'"

The claims were salacious, and their source, an escort with seemingly little to lose, led to understandable skepticism. But Powell's tales were true. One of the recruits who was at the parties, and ultimately did not choose Louisville, told ESPN's *Outside the Lines,* "I knew they weren't college girls. It was crazy. It was like I was in a strip club."

The parties were not a onetime thing; they occurred periodically over the course of four years, between 2010 and 2014. They took place in Billy Minardi Hall, a dormitory named for Pitino's brother-in-law and best friend, who worked for Cantor Fitzgerald and died at the World Trade Center on September 11, 2001.

Even by the gutter standards of NCAA scandals—the serial personal and institutional misconduct that is a regular staple of sports news—this was about as bad as it gets. Sex parties involving paid escorts. In the basketball dorm. Sponsored by a key employee of the head coach's. The revelations called into question Pitino's leadership. He claimed not to know anything about the parties—but how did he not know that someone working right under him had such shockingly poor judgment? Was McGee really a model employee except for those four years of sex parties he arranged?

That the parties went on where the players lived also reflected something about the culture of Louisville's basketball program. Was there not a single player who thought to raise an objection? Or one who thought to tell Pitino directly, or at least find a way to get word to him, that there were some activities going on that didn't seem quite right and that might not look good in the light of day if they became public? Or did the players just assume that since McGee worked closely with Pitino, their head coach knew about the parties and approved?

The NCAA launched an investigation, and in June 2017 its Committee on Infractions issued its report. "The COI has not previously encountered a case like this," it began, which seemed like a rare bit of wit on the part of the NCAA. "A member of the men's basketball staff arranged on-campus striptease dances and acts of prostitution for enrolled student-athletes and prospective student-athletes, some of whom were minors, on their campus visits."

Louisville's own internal investigation confirmed the truth of most of Katina Powell's story. Where the university differed with the NCAA was that it did not believe there was a great deal of institutional blame to go around—and none that attached to Pitino. That was likely Jurich's influence, the lesson he learned from his father: loyalty above all else.

But that kind of backing was also what the thin-skinned Pitino demanded. He did not accept blame, he shifted it. If the university had found him at all culpable in the Strippergate affair, he would have thrown a fit. "With a few minor exceptions, [Louisville] agreed that the striptease dances and prostitution occurred," the NCAA said. "The institution and the head men's basketball coach did not agree that the facts established the head men's basketball coach failed to monitor the former director of men's basketball operations."

How could Pitino possibly be completely absolved of sex parties sponsored by his employee, in the basketball dorm, involving some of his players? Wasn't that at the very least a hiring issue? An issue with his ability to communicate the values of his organization?

The NCAA, in certain extreme cases, "vacates" victories. It is an

Orwellian term and act—a way of reaching back and erasing history. Louisville's stirring victory over Michigan on April 8, 2013, in Atlanta was vacated, along with its national championship. Luke Hancock was no longer the tournament's most outstanding player. Kevin Ware, the substitute who broke his leg against Duke, could no longer consider himself a national champion, or at least not according to the NCAA. The title was not given over to Michigan. Instead, it was as if the game was never played. The tournament in 2013 had no champion.

Louisville and Pitino were stripped of 123 victories earned in the four years the parties were taking place, and the NCAA ordered the university to remove any references to the wins or championships "from athletics department stationery, banners displayed in public areas and any other forum in which they may appear."

Pitino's 770 career victories ranked fifteenth among all men's Division I coaches, an impressive total, especially considering that he had gone off to coach in the NBA for six seasons. Even at sixty-five years old, he still had plenty of passion and energy left, so if he kept coaching he would have climbed the list. He likely could not have caught Mike Krzyzewski, Duke's still-active "Coach K," but the retired coaches in the top five—Bob Knight, Dean Smith, and Adolph Rupp—were within Pitino's reach.

But after the NCAA vacated his victories, Pitino fell all the way down to thirty-seventh on the all-time list—below coaches he had surpassed like Hank Iba and Phog Allen, pioneers from basketball's early days; below UCLA's John Wooden, the sainted Wizard of Westwood; below UNLV's Jerry Tarkanian, who had his own famous battles with the NCAA; and also below his predecessor at Louisville, Denny Crum.

Pitino applies a sort of circular logic in times when he is accused of wrongdoing. He could not have broken rules because he is a person who is well known for having great respect for the rules. Everyone around him knows how he feels, because he tells them time and time again: Follow the rules. When people who work closely with him break the rules, they do not tell him about it—and in fact go to great lengths to hide their misbehaviors—because they know how angry he would be. It is therefore understandable that some bad stuff might happen on his watch without him knowing about it.

This is not a model of crisis response you would find recommended in any leadership book—most of those tend to follow a philosophy of "the buck stops here"—but it is one that worked well for Pitino as the coach of Louisville basketball. When the NCAA announced its sanctions and stripped his teams of their victories and the 2013 national title, he was filled with umbrage, outrage, and grievance, which he expressed in a letter sent to Louisville fans. It was addressed, "Dear Friends of the 'Ville."

"When the news first came out in 2015," he wrote, referring to the revelations in Katina Powell's book, "it sunk my emotions to the lowest point anyone could possibly imagine. I write this letter to tell you and encourage you to keep your spirits high." The NCAA, he said, had been unduly harsh and he supported the university's decision to appeal the penalties.

By the time the news of the sex parties broke, Andre McGee had moved on from the Louisville staff and was an assistant coach at the University of Missouri–Kansas City. He left that job in the wake of the scandal and was later reportedly driving an Uber. He has never talked publicly about the parties in Billy Minardi Hall or revealed the source of the $10,000 that was paid for the dancers. In Pitino's letter, he laid the blame entirely on McGee, who played four seasons for him and was Louisville's starting point guard as a senior, in 2008–09.

"Let me clear up the following and leave no doubt that this is the truth and the only truth," Pitino wrote. "Billy Minardi Hall was built in memory of my best friend and brother-in-law who I lost on 9/11. If I knew of anything that was going on there that would dishonor his name, that person wouldn't be able to get out of town fast enough.

"I was told during the process that I didn't ask pointed questions. Well what does that mean exactly? I asked our staff if the recruits enjoyed themselves. What did they do? How did they like everything? I then met with their families for breakfast and asked the same questions. No, I did not ask the staff if they saw any strippers last night. I can assure you that if I asked Andre any difficult question, he would have lied to my face to avoid immediate termination."

There were fewer than forty residents of Billy Minardi Hall, all of them either players or in some way connected to the basketball program. The all-male residence is built for larger-than-average human beings and includes such amenities as extra-tall standup showers and queen-sized beds. Meals are prepared by a personal chef.

Pitino said he asked around to coaches and players, past and present, and all reported that they knew nothing about the strippers in the dorm. Somehow, at least fourteen parties had taken place, but they escaped the notice of everyone who was not involved. There were strippers and escorts with young men in their late teens and early twenties, but everyone was very, very quiet.

Pitino ascribed a high degree of cleverness to McGee, as if having parties in such a setting and keeping them quiet was on a par with complex and difficult-to-discover Wall Street malfeasance. He referred to what happened in his basketball dorm as "the greatest hidden thing I've ever witnessed in my lifetime." When he asked around afterward, no one had even had a hint of the escapades. "Bernie Madoff fooled the smartest people on Wall Street, SEC, family, brokers and major hedge funds," his letter said. "There are no questions that I asked to even give me a small clue to what was going on. Security employees, managers, assistant coaches, fellow students and most importantly, Billy Minardi's children, and my nephews, all lived in that dorm. They were all questioned by me, and not one had any suspicion of any inappropriate activities going on in that dormitory."

At a press conference, Pitino suggested that an NCAA probe may have led to the death of former North Carolina State coach Jim Valvano, who died at forty-seven years old of cancer. He recalled a conversation in which Valvano told him that an ongoing NCAA investigation "broke down my immune system."

"And I always thought about that," Pitino said. "It can kill you inside because you know what you stand for and believe in. So what do you do? Do you say, 'Let me pack it in. Let me do something else in life'? Leaders lead. I plan on staying here and winning multiple championships, not just one. I plan on going to multiple Final Fours, not just one. And that's what leaders do. They lead the players they're coaching."

There were several junctures when Louisville might have broken with Pitino—when the revelations first surfaced in the fall of 2015; early in 2016, when the university's own probe led it to "self-impose" penalties and sit out the NCAA tournament that spring; in the fall of 2016, when the NCAA released its report; or that summer of 2017, when it imposed the sanctions. But Jurich and the university administration stood by him.

After the NCAA announced its penalties, Jurich pointed out that there was never even a hint of the parties around the time they were happening. He fell in line with Pitino's thinking—that no one else in the program knew about the parties and that their secret nature was nothing short of miraculous. "How did social media never have one release on this?" he said when we talked in Colorado. "I look for red flags all the time . . . too much of the time, because I'm so protective of this program. But this one got by me, too."

Pitino and Jurich had one big clash. It came in 2014, as Jurich was in the process of hiring a new football coach—one who had the distinction of being just about the only other coach in the NCAA as sexually scandalized as Pitino. (They also happened to have a last name that rhymed.) While he was head coach at Arkansas, Bobby Petrino crashed his motorcycle on a country highway and initially neglected to tell police he had someone riding on the back—a twenty-five-year-old former volleyball player at the university and an employee on the football staff. After details spilled out that she was the then fifty-one-year-old Petrino's mistress, he was fired.

Petrino was a polarizing figure on several counts, including the fact that he switched jobs frequently and sometimes abruptly, leaving employers in the lurch. The website SB Nation ran a story in

2016 with the headline "The Bobby Petrino Controversy Timeline: 15 Years of Shenanigans."

Petrino, however, was an acknowledged offensive genius—just the kind of football coach favored by Jurich. He won. He put fans in the seats. And he got donors excited. He had two previous stints at Louisville—as an assistant to John L. Smith and then as head coach between 2003 and 2006. He was coaching at Western Kentucky after Arkansas fired him, so a return to Louisville represented a step back into major college football.

Pitino did not object to Petrino's hiring on any moral basis—what he feared was that it would dredge up discussion of his own indiscretion with Karen Sypher. "Jurich showed no interest in the character of his coaches," Tim Sullivan, the *Louisville Courier-Journal* sports columnist, said. "When he hired Petrino back, this was five years or so past the Karen Sypher trial. It was remembered but it wasn't like it was in the news every day. The word was that Rick was apoplectic. He was measured in his public comments, but underneath that, he was seething. Jurich basically told him, 'Mind your own business. I had your back when you needed it. I'll hire who I want.'"

A former trustee at the university who was in on the discussions over Petrino's hiring confirms that Rick Pitino raised objections. "Yes, Rick was pissed. He thought it would all come back on him. Tom Jurich had counseled Petrino after the Arkansas thing. He told him what he had to do to get himself back in at this level. Jurich and Pitino had a meeting and Tom told him, 'This is what I'm doing. It's my call to make, not yours.' Pitino is smart. He learns and grows. He apologized and made his peace with it.

"There's two ways to look at it. It can be argued that athletics is the bastion of liberalism and second chances. That's not a bad thing. It's a benign explanation. The other way to see it is that for some reason, we had two coaches of our highest-profile athletic programs with bad personal habits."

Said Terry Meiners, "Rick was marking his territory and trying to make it clear this was his universe. He didn't like the mess Petrino had left behind in Arkansas. It made him uncomfortable because he felt like it was going to reflect back on him."

Pitino did not go back to Porcini much after the Karen Sypher trial in 2009. His restaurant of choice became Jeff Ruby's in downtown Louisville, a big, bustling place with a lively bar and a well-heeled clientele. It is a non–New Yorker's idea of a buzzy New York restaurant. A pianist sits on an elevated platform above the bar, playing show tunes and popular music on a black-lacquered piano (you could count on someone just about every night requesting "New York, New York"). Pitino usually sat at a table with friends in the front room, and sometimes would finish the evening with a last glass of wine at the bar.

He referenced his transgression at Porcini periodically, more than you would imagine—usually when his own conduct or the conduct of his program came into question. It was part of his personal narrative, his testimony, as it were, that he answered to a higher power than the NCAA. His point was clear: You couldn't criticize him—and certainly could not render a moral judgment—because God was already doing that.

In his letter to Louisville fans after the wins and national title were vacated, he wrote, "Over twelve years ago, I hurt my wife and family by doing some improper things. I paid a heavy price with

them and The Lord. We, as a family, are closer today than ever before and my faith is stronger than at any point in my life. I'm in this
game for one reason, and only for one reason: to teach young men
how to reach their potential on and off the court.

"You, our loyal Louisville family, can rest assured we believe in
doing the right thing and doing things that are important in the
eyes of God."

CHAPTER SIX

FISHING IN POLLUTED WATERS

The relentless hum of commercial activity around NCAA sports, and the never-ending push for more and bigger deals, is part of the Sonny Vaccaro legacy. College sport is a nakedly money-seeking endeavor, and no one even bothers to pretend otherwise. It all runs on a parallel track to the games themselves, as another arena for competition and scorekeeping.

The rationale is that everyone is in the grip of a never-ending "arms race"—a competition to erect the most gilded facilities in order to attract the highest-level recruits. Mahogany-paneled locker rooms. Extra-large, individualized shower stalls. Training facilities that match or even exceed the level of NBA and NFL franchises. Amphitheaters with stadium seating to watch game film.

It is all self-fulfilling logic. If your facilities are dingy, top re-cruits will in fact walk away—if they even bother to visit at all. But once you build this kind of stuff, the implications of a couple of bad recruiting years are catastrophic. It is untenable to raise money for first-rate facilities and then attract second-rate athletes. You lose the arms race. You're annihilated.

The *Portland Business Journal* energetically covers its home-town company, Nike, and has taken a broad interest in the sources of money that flow into NCAA sports. It tracks advertising deals on campuses, which are mostly controlled by two companies, IMG College and Learfield, that pay lump sums to athletic programs for the right to sell space. One reason why commercial interests like college sports is that universities will sell just about any flat space for advertising purposes. Unlike professional franchises, which are limited by deals the leagues have cut with national advertisers, col-lege venues are blank canvases and wide open for business.

IMG College, which represents some seventy-five universities, embeds teams of its own employees on campuses, where they func-tion as outside advertising agencies working from within university athletic departments. The company's deal with UCLA authorizes it to sell "official" and "exclusive" designations such as the "official bank of UCLA athletics" and the "official water." It can sell signage on scoreboards, video boards, press row signs, courtside signs, chair backs, basketball backboard stations, shot clocks, team entry tarpaulins, and cup holders on seats. In football, it markets space on the nets that kickers boot balls into on the sidelines.

In addition, "miscellaneous" advertising opportunities include schedule cards, posters, ticket backs, roster cards, media guides, ticket mailer inserts, ticket envelopes, cups, coolers, towels, and wa-ter bottles. The contract prohibits IMG from selling advertising for a range of unwholesome products, including tobacco, escort services, and male enhancement supplements. (Incongruously, "female hygiene products" are also on the banned list, as if advertising for them would somehow detract from the experience of watching a college sporting event.)

Pro football is by far the most popular sport in America (even with its declining TV ratings in recent seasons), but its viewers are not as attractive to advertisers as some might imagine. The NFL has more overall viewers, but "a less enviable demographic than college football and basketball," says Jonathan Jensen, a sports marketing professor at the University of North Carolina. "The majority of people watching NFL games did not go to college and they have lower incomes than the college audience. They're a less coveted consumer."

College football is number two in the annual popularity surveys conducted by Rich Luker, a social psychologist who has been conducting the annual ESPN Sports Poll since 1994. Next comes the NBA, and right after that (and before Major League Baseball) is college basketball. The people most interested in college sports tend to be "more educated, which means they have more disposable income," Jensen says.

Current college students represent another coveted demographic. They are going to earn more money than their less-educated peers—and they are at an impressionable age and just starting to establish their buying habits and brand loyalties.

The partnerships between athletic departments and Nike, Adidas, and Under Armour represent an even bigger bargain for companies than the advertising deals. Much of the reported value of the contracts is delivered in shoes, uniforms, wristbands, and other accessories worn by student-athletes, rather than cash, thereby turning college athletes into a combination of action figures and billboards. Because of their deals with universities, Jensen said, "Nike and the other apparel companies now barely need to advertise. Their logo is on the uniforms and all over the place.

"They have 99.9 percent brand awareness. Procter and Gamble spends $8 billion across its brands per year on advertising. Nike does not. They don't need it. These agreements are their media buys. It saves them a tremendous amount of money."

The endemic criminal and ethical scandals of college sports are connected by a straight line to the money. Teams that do not win do not excite their boosters, fill up stadiums, appear on national TV, or get into postseason play, thereby endangering the revenue stream that supports the immense infrastructure. It is the desperation for cash, every bit as much as the pursuit of victory, that causes universities to overlook all kinds of rule-breaking until it splatters out into the open. At that point, they may try to manage their problems, but they can never really address the root causes.

The most egregious example in recent years has been Baylor University, a Southern Baptist school that plays in the highly competitive (and lucrative) Big 12 Conference. In 2003, a member of its basketball team murdered a teammate. The ensuing investigation led to revelations of drug and alcohol use on the team, payments to players, and (of course) flagrant recruiting violations.

In 2016, it became clear that Baylor coaches and others knew about but ignored serious allegations of sexual assault by its football players, including one that led to a criminal conviction and twenty-year prison sentence. An investigation by an outside law firm hired by Baylor uncovered at least nineteen incidents of alleged sexual assaults by players that were reported by seventeen different women.

The two Baylor scandals led to coaches, athletic directors, and university administrators losing their jobs. (Kenneth Starr, the Baylor president and former special prosecutor of President Bill Clinton, was demoted in the wake of the 2016 scandal, and then resigned.) The scandals caused Baylor's teams to be hobbled by NCAA sanctions, but the university has not reappraised its ambitions. No one, seemingly, ever asks: Are our aspirations part of the problem? The cycle of raising money, recruiting players, and seeking bigger shoe deals and more generous corporate partners continues, presumably until the next scandal hits. And beyond.

The same could be said of numerous NCAA programs caught in wrongdoing, including North Carolina, where for two decades athletes took advantage of a "shadow curriculum" of what were called fake classes to get grades and stay eligible. Many required no attendance and just one paper. The whole thing seemed like an obvious violation of NCAA rules and an affront to the notion of the "student-athlete."

But the NCAA threaded a legalistic needle to let North Carolina and its admired basketball program—where Dean Smith coached and Michael Jordan played—escape penalties. It ruled that because the sham classes were in theory available to any students who knew about them and presumably did not mind wasting their tuition money, they did not constitute impermissible benefits specifically designed for athletes. The NCAA's reprieve for UNC came six months after the Tar Heels men's basketball team won the national championship, their sixth.

Even schools that are penalized experience sanctions as only a speed bump. In 2016, when Baylor introduced its new football coach, Matt Rhule, he spoke in a string of exclamation points. "We're going to play great defense!" he proclaimed. "We're going to have a dynamic offense! We want to be a team that makes everybody proud! When you watch us play, I want you to say to yourselves, 'That's my team!'" He promised to build a championship team, and concluded, as he walked off the podium, by shouting the Baylor slogan: "Sic 'em Bears!"

The values of NCAA sports percolate down to the youth level. Grassroots basketball players understand that they are involved in a commercial enterprise, not a game. It is not unusual to hear a high school player, or even a middle schooler, talk about how the "business" of basketball works, and they are not referring to the NBA. They well understand that the driving force of their sport is not fun or youth development or education. It's money.

More than three hundred pre–high school boys were gathered in San Diego for the Junior Phenom Camp, a national showcase of players who had earned their way there via regional events. Most of them paid $450 to participate, which came from either their family, their youth team, a sneaker company, or some other benefactor. (I attended the camp several years ago, on assignment for the *New York Times Magazine*.) The stars, the highest ranked of the competitors, played for free and were flown in by the camp's organizer. They gave the Junior Phenom Camp its luster. All the other players wanted to improve on their rankings, and they couldn't do that unless the top kids showed up.

The event was categorized as an "exposure camp" to distinguish it from camps whose primary mission is teaching, but the players were really performing for an audience of one: Clark Francis, the editor of the Hoop Scoop, an online tout sheet, many of whose subscribers are either college coaches or parents who want to see how their kids measure up. Francis was the first to assign national rankings to very young players, to the point that you will see on his site such notations as "our ranking of the top seven 5th graders." To his credit, the evaluations are not pie-in-the-sky guesses—if you look through the Hoop Scoop's past rankings of grade schoolers, you'll find dozens of significant college and NBA players. It is evidence of his and other talent evaluators' ability to identify hoops prodigies. Karl-Anthony Towns, now seven feet tall and one of the NBA's best young players, first shows up on the Hoop Scoop radar as a five-foot-nine fifth grader. The Hoop Scoop identified Trae Young, one of the leading players in college basketball in 2017, as a five-foot-four sixth grader.

Without the presence of Francis, the camp would have lost its edge and a chunk of its paying clientele. "They all know that Clark Francis is going to be here" is how the camp director, Joe Keller, explained. "They know coming in, you're going to get evaluated, you're going to get ranked. That's part of the branding. Without it, we wouldn't get players. But we get the best players, and they get what they pay for."

A certain kind of sports obsessive likes to feel in the know—that he has seen, or even just heard of, some up-and-coming player before the rest of the world has caught on. A whole industry grew up around so-called NFL draftniks, men (and they are just about all men) who keep track of not just the top projected picks in the annual spring draft, but also the obscure offensive lineman from some out-of-the-way school who might get picked up in the sixth or seventh round. In basketball, the clock is set much earlier, in large part because of LeBron James, who was such a known talent from his early teens that his first high school game, in ninth grade, was eagerly anticipated by insiders. The televising of high school games took off during the four years James was prepping for the NBA at St. Vincent–St. Mary High School in Akron, and the explosion in basketball interest below the high school level, and much of the money that courses through it, is directly related to him.

Francis, the Hoop Scoop editor, is a man of strong opinions and snap judgments. "It's not PC what I do, ranking young kids," he said. "I know that. Some people like it, some people don't. But if you're playing at an event and I'm not scouting it, nobody knows and nobody cares." He laid out what he was looking for in players this young: "Size, athleticism, outside shooting. Bottom line is, if you don't have one of those things, forget it. Go play soccer. Have a nice life."

The boys at the Phenom Camp were put on teams that played twice a day, on one of six full courts in a cavernous gymnasium at Alliant International University that was as big as an airplane hangar. Presiding over everything was Keller, the camp director, a former AAU coach in Southern California and the president of the company that ran the camp as well as a web of other similar events in the United States, Canada, Puerto Rico, Japan, and China. "Have you seen No. 109?" he observed at one point as he watched the action on one of the courts. "He's a monster, isn't he?" He was referring to a sixth grader who played for an AAU team based in Houston that had competed in 118 games in the previous twelve months—36 games more than the NBA's regular season. The boy lived down in the Rio Grande Valley, nearly four hundred miles away, but flew to Houston to join his teammates for one of their rare practices or to meet them at the airport to set off on road trips.

A moment later, the camp director's attention was drawn to another sixth grader, a smaller but highly skilled player. "Going to be a pro," Keller said. "You mark my word."

Everyone seemed to know this kid had a six-foot-eleven father and assumed he just had not yet hit his growth spurt. It's something that basketball aficionados always clock: the size of a kid's parents. If the father is not on the scene, they just ask the mom: How tall is his dad?

The most exalted of the campers was a sixth grader named Alonzo Trier, who lived in Federal Way, Washington, outside Seattle, and had his own line of clothing emblazoned with his signature and personal motto: "When the lights come on, it's time to perform." His basketball socks were marked with either his nickname, Zo, or his area code, 206. (He was then too young to fall under NCAA rules governing the benefits an athlete being recruited could receive.) Francis was enamored of Trier—he loved his game and his dedication to the sport. He always called Trier by his first and last name, as a sign of respect. "Allonzo Trier is going to make it no matter what," he said. "And that's what makes Allonzo Trier fun to watch. He just does things right."

The father of another camper tapped Trier on the shoulder between games and asked if he would pose for a picture with his son. "Thank you," he said to him after snapping the photo. "You're a role model, brother."

The only child of a social-worker single mother, Trier would spend the next half dozen years bouncing between AAU teams in Seattle, Dallas, and Tulsa, and private high schools with prominent basketball programs in Oklahoma City, suburban Washington, D.C., and Las Vegas. These were not relocations occasioned by his mother's work or other family considerations. They were career moves, driven by basketball. Better opportunities on the grassroots scene.

It's not unusual for young players and their families to pick up and move in order to change high school or AAU teams, although Trier, who went on to play for the University of Arizona, was one of the more extreme examples. When the *Washington Post* wrote about his journey, it headlined the story, "Allonzo Trier Is a Complicated Case of Free Agency in Elite High School."

All kinds of merchandise was on sale for purchase at the Phenom Camp, including a camp program for $25 that listed the participants and their heights, hobbies, hometowns, and nicknames. The monikers they chose revealed all you needed to know about the milieu in which young basketball talent is identified and nurtured. There was a G-Money, a K-Money, a Cash-Money, and one young man who simply called himself Money. Two campers went by Sir, while others also had handles that seemed to demand respect—Da Truth, Superstar, Big Dog, and the Chosen One.

The attention directed at young talent by Clark Francis and others makes the best of the players magnets and attracts opportunists who swoop in and attach themselves to kids and their families. "You have runners, street agents, and advisors right from the jump," says a veteran assistant coach who has worked at top programs in several different conferences. "You have sixth graders with advisors. Advising on what? How the fuck does a kid in the sixth grade need an advisor? The kid is twelve years old. He still watches cartoons. What's your advice? Stop watching cartoons? Watch better cartoons? That's what we deal with when we're recruiting—a kid who's had a circus around him for four, five, or six years. That's his life and it seems normal to him. People think we corrupt these kids.

But that's not how it is. There's shit that's already been going on since way before we get on to him.

"The advisor, he doesn't have any advice that's worth listening to. His role is get himself embedded with the family and take credit when the gear from the shoe companies starts coming. He says, 'I did that.' Maybe he tries to get more stuff and he spreads it around to other kids he's working on. The payoff he's angling for is to be there when the real money starts coming. He's a parasite, pure and simple."

A t all the major college basketball programs, a head coach has three assistants on his staff, along with a "director of basketball operations" who functions as a coach but without the title, an athletic trainer and a couple of assistant trainers, strength and conditioning coaches, a video coordinator, a half dozen or so student managers, and various other administrators and staffers. There is a maximum of thirteen players under scholarship at any given time, but easily four times that number to serve their needs and keep the program moving forward—which includes acquiring players for future seasons.

Recruiting is an obsessive year-round pursuit for coaches who are intensely, if not pathologically, competitive. They have ascended to their jobs for a variety of reasons, and one of them is that they want to win more than normal people do. Men with hundreds of career victories and multiple titles still feel after losses as if the life has been sucked out of them.

Recruiting for these coaches is another game in that it only has two possible outcomes: A win or a loss. Life or death. Their egos are in play, perhaps even more so than during athletic competition.

Having set their sights on recruits, often for many years—having made calls and visits and sent dozens of letters and texts—they feel personally rejected when a high school player chooses another suitor.

Landing a top prospect is as much about winning the recruiting battle as it is about actually coaching him. In both college football and basketball, recruiting does not stop during the season, and in fact takes on a measure of importance that rivals game preparation. I spent a week with Pete Carroll, coach of the NFL's Seattle Seahawks, back when he was head football coach at the University of Southern California. His team had just suffered a surprising loss to Oregon State and had an important game upcoming against Ohio State. After practices, Carroll and his assistants ate dinner together out of plastic takeout containers in a common room at the center of their office suite and spent an hour making phone calls to high school kids.

"How you doin' academically? You keepin' up with your class-work?" Carroll asked one recruit. When he was done with his conversation, he passed the phone to another coach. "Coach Sark wants to talk with you," he said, referring to his then assistant Steve Sarkisian. Carroll dialed up another recruit and talked to him, and then asked for his mother. "Hey Mom, what's happenin'?" he said when she got on the phone. The cell phones got passed around like they were part of some multiple handoff play as each coach got a kid on the phone, started a conversation, and then brought in another staff member. I was struck that even on such an important week, and following an upset loss, recruiting retained its high priority. But the talent pipeline must constantly be replenished.

As the college basketball season is under way, coaches are

looking toward the next season and the one after that. LeBron James went right from high school to the NBA in 2003, which is no longer permitted. The rule change in 2005 that players had to be at least nineteen years old and one year out of high school ushered in the current "one-and-done" era. Now the best young players, and the objects of the most fevered recruiting, often play just one season and are on campus for no more than nine months. For the coaches who ardently recruited them, they get to compete for all of five months.

At the top programs that lose multiple underclassmen each year to the NBA and must replenish, recruiting is especially intense and high-stakes. If a coach loses three or four of his kids to the NBA draft and doesn't have a good recruiting cycle, he is basically left without a team. That prospect—the cupboard stripped bare, a losing record in the conference, no NCAA tourney bid—is never far from his mind.

Top coaches fly to visit recruits at their homes on private jets, paid for by the university or lent by wealthy boosters. In sales terms, they are the closers. The day-to-day, constant pressure of recruiting falls to the assistant coaches. They follow kids from their early teens on up (sometimes after they end up on one of Clark Francis's lists) and develop relationships long before a program is sure it wants to extend a scholarship offer.

To demonstrate interest, they show up at as many games and all-star events as they can—often during periods when the NCAA does not permit them to talk to recruits or their families but does allow them to scout. "I was like a sandwich board," a veteran assistant says. "I would position myself under the basket where a kid is warming up. I've got my shirt, my hat, my pants—everything's got the school's colors and logo—I want to be seen by the kid. He knows I'm there looking at him. He thinks to himself, 'There's three hundred coaches in the gym, but this guy, he really wants me.'"

A crucial role of the assistant coach is to function as an intelligence gatherer: How big is the entourage around the kid? Who's the decision maker? The mom, the dad, an uncle, an advisor, a high school or AAU coach? They need to find out if a player's family is seeking money or other benefits not permitted by the NCAA. A program that pays will want to know how much. The ones that don't will walk away.

There's an adage in recruiting that the best answer is "yes" and the second best is "no." The worst is "maybe," because coaches do not want to be strung along or used as leverage by a player seeking a better deal elsewhere.

Few coaches currently working in college basketball, or hoping to get back in, are willing to be quoted by name. A former assistant coach at a Big Ten school tells the following story:

"I was involved with a kid and I get a call from his AAU coach, and he says, 'Just to let you know, the starting price for him is room and board for his family,' meaning they wanted to move to the college town and be set up with living arrangements. I said, 'Thanks for letting me know,' and I really meant that. We weren't going to provide that, so I was really glad he told me what they wanted.

"It's not always overt. Things are hinted at and you get the idea. But sometimes it's so overt that it blows you away and you think to yourself, 'Did I just hear that?' We had one kid verbally commit to us, and the next thing you know, he shows up on campus with a guy we had never seen before and this guy says, 'So how does it work? You set up an LLC in a name that we give you, and put the money into that?' We said no, and the kid decommitted. He went somewhere else and I assume they got the money they were looking for. I don't know if he got it in an LLC or not."

T om Konchalski was one of the first of what are now commonly called recruiting gurus. He is seventy-two years old, a six-foot-six former high school basketball player (he says he was not particularly good) and a lifelong bachelor who works from his apartment in Queens when he is not traveling to see games. He composes his recruiting reports on a typewriter and mails copies to coaches who subscribe to his service. He does not use a cell phone or computer, and perhaps as a result, his memory is especially sharp. When we were setting up a meeting, he asked if there was a casual spot to talk near where I was staying in Manhattan. When I suggested the Chelsea Diner, he said, "I know that place. Southeast corner of 23rd and Ninth."

Konchalski, who has a philosophy degree from Fordham, is a gentleman in an elbows-out business. A *New York Times* profile once described him as a combination of concerned priest and military dad, and the sportswriter John Feinstein referred to him as "the last honest man in the gym." He is not, however, naïve. He began following college basketball when it was a niche sport and he had to watch NCAA tournament games on tape delay on local stations, or not at all if a New York–area team was not involved. "There's so much more money now, which means more temptation," he says. "It's coming in from every direction. The NCAA has never been able to police it, and I don't know how hard they've tried. So now you have something that I don't think anyone ever expected—the FBI being involved."

Konchalski and others stressed the pressure assistant coaches are under to deliver players, and the challenge of dealing in a realm in which families have been getting paid in various ways and by various sources, for years.

An NBA scout with long-standing connections in the grassroots scene explained how it works. "You have families that when their kid gets good, the parents stop working. They've got a million people telling them their son is going to be in the NBA and they believe it because it's their first time around the block. They don't have any objective measure to weigh it against. Their life becomes the AAU scene, camps, private training. If they didn't need money before, they do now, because they have no income."

There is a progression of benefits to families. In the beginning, the grade school years, it is boxes of sneakers and gear and maybe hotel rooms and dinners when their son is traveling with his AAU team. Eventually, the NBA scout said, the "runners"—proxies acting on behalf of agents—"and the financial advisors and college coaches come around. In the worst-case scenario, they're all working together. The runner brings in the coaches—or one of the assistant coaches brings in the runner. You have to understand, these people all work together. It's one world. It doesn't seem wrong to them. They share intelligence. They have common interests.

"The family gets a car. Then some money. When it comes time to commit to a college, you've been taking money at every step along the way, so there's absolutely no rationale to stop. Has the kid gotten any of it? Probably not, or not much."

Coaches who outright bribe recruits to attend—and no one denies that there are some—face the challenge of teaching, mentoring, and, if necessary, disciplining players whom they have lured illicitly. They're in a dirty deal together. The traditional role of a coach—leader of young men, instiller of values, builder of character—is subverted. "Can they be coached if the coach broke the rules to get them there?" Konchalski says. "Sometimes not. But I've seen it both ways. If there's a point of intersection of mutual self-interest, yes. When the kid truly wants to improve, he'll accept coaching, even from a coach who paid to get him there."

The top grassroots players have already been playing under AAU coaches who may have profited off their talent. Nike's circuit of top AAU players consists of forty teams around the nation (it's known as the EYBL, for Elite Youth Basketball League) that play a national schedule and a series of tournaments in the spring. Adidas operates a grassroots tournament called the Gauntlet, and Under Armour's goes by the UA Association. The shoe companies contribute as much as $300,000 to some of these individual clubs, which operate as nonprofits. The case announced by the Justice Department in September 2017 implies that shoe companies use the clubs as pass-throughs, sending money to the clubs that is then sometimes funneled to players or their families.

The shoe companies also engage in another way to get money to the families of sought-after high school players, one that, at least technically, does not seem to violate NCAA rules: Rather than secretly funnel it through a third party like Christian Dawkins, they just fund an AAU team that is operated by a top prospect's parents. Marvin Bagley III, who played the 2017–18 season at Duke before turning pro, competed for the youth team Phoenix Phamily, which was started by his father, Marvin Bagley Jr., when his son was in his mid-teens—and funded by Nike. His father told *Sports Illustrated* in 2016 that the Nike money was helping his family "make ends meet."

Apples Jones, the mother of 2016–17 Kansas player Josh Jackson, founded the 1Nation AAU program at the same time that her son was the object of intense recruiting attention. It was funded by Under Armour, and her son signed on as an endorser with the company just before the 2017 NBA draft. "I am thrilled to officially be a part of team Under Armour as I start my professional career," he said. He praised Under Armour as "a leading force in basketball today."

Steve Haney, the lawyer for Christian Dawkins, is a former college basketball player whose son played AAU and Division I basketball. Of all the lawyers involved in the federal case, on the prosecution or defense, he is the most well versed on the grassroots scene. "You've got these companies funding whole AAU programs run by kids' families," he says. "It's at least a couple of hundred thousand dollars. It could be more. I honestly don't get it. Can anyone tell me the difference between that and what my client is accused of?"

The shoe company money is intended to buy fealty to the brand. The hope is that a young player will progress from one of their AAU teams, to a college program they sponsor, and then, if they become a pro, to wearing their gear in the NBA. In 2014, Rick Pitino lamented that he had a smaller pool of prospects to recruit from because of Louisville's connection to Adidas, which sponsors fewer grassroots programs than Nike does. When he was asked if there were other coaches who did not like the system, he said, "I'm sure the Nike coaches don't feel that way because they're winning the battle."

Players often, but not always, choose a college team that wears the same shoes as their grassroots program. "It's what the shoe companies want," Konchalski said. "But it depends on the leverage their AAU coach has on a player."

The veteran assistant coach says, "If the family needs money, the sneaker companies are going to offer. If it's offered, the family is going to take it. Is that clear enough? As a coach, you have to ask, 'What river am I fishing in? What lake?' Some of the fish in there are polluted. Do you want to eat that fish? Are you going to get sick if you do? Is the program going to get sick? This is the scene. You can't change the scene. You make your little choices within it.

"The head coach says to you, 'Who the fuck do you have for me today? Go get me players.' But at what cost? My job? Your job? Do I go to the sneaker guy? The boosters? To you? There's a middle ground between what you do and what the head coach does—what he knows about what you're doing and what he doesn't want to know. A lot of them want that middle ground to be as big as possible.

"Sonny Vaccaro is the godfather of all this. He didn't intend what happened. It got out of his control. The shoe companies are recruiting kids just like the college programs are, but they're in there first. That's the underbelly of this thing. The PC term is 'grassroots' basketball. It's really a hunting ground—a hunting ground for street agents and leeches. The money has floated down to younger and younger kids and created expectations, and we're the bad guys either way. We're either the cheaters who pay kids or we're the guys saying to families, 'We want your kid but, no, no, the spigot just stopped. We want him for free.'"

FBI investigators, armed with court-ordered wiretaps, listened in on exchanges that coaches and others assumed were private, about two hundred hours of recorded phone conversations taken from some thirteen hundred calls that were deemed "pertinent," meaning the participants were talking about matters the FBI considered relevant to its probe. In addition, undercover agents and cooperating witnesses secretly videotaped more than two dozen meetings in hotel rooms, restaurants, and airports. The highlights of these—enough to support the indictments—have been revealed, but much more is coming.

The day the FBI arrested the coaches and others, the veteran assistant said, was a moment of extreme panic across the college basketball landscape. As he put it, "There's what, 350-some Division I programs? Believe me, at least half of them had staff meetings that day because they needed to find out: Who's the touch? Who's the guy on our staff that mixed with some of these people? Where's the one degree of separation? College basketball is a small world. I'm talking about the coaches, runners, kids, uncles, agents, scouting gurus, financial advisors, you name it. Everybody knows everybody. We all live together in a broom closet, so there's always that touch."

The lucrative salaries paid to college coaches are probably not news to most people who closely follow sports. Coaches are often the highest-paid public employees in their states, with salaries dwarfing those of governors, college presidents, deans of medical schools, renowned researchers, and all other top talent at their institutions. At least fourteen head college basketball coaches earn more than $3 million a year. The total is likely higher, because salaries are reported in various ways in different states and at private and public institutions, and add-ons like life insurance policies and various bonuses are not always revealed. According to numbers compiled by *USA Today,* Rick Pitino, before he was fired, was the top-paid basketball coach in 2016–17 at $7.8 million annually. In the newspaper's last survey of salaries, pay hikes had elevated two coaches above that figure—Duke coach Mike Krzyzewski was making $8.98 million and Kentucky's John Calipari $8 million. NCAA football coaches make even bigger salaries, with Alabama's Nick Saban, who made $11 million in 2017, leading the pack.

The generous deals given to assistant coaches may be a little more surprising. Lamont Evans, one of the four assistant coaches indicted in the federal case, was making $600,000 a year at Oklahoma State. Louisville's Kenny Johnson was earning $550,000. The youngest of Pitino's assistants, Jordan Fair, twenty-eight, who was just two years removed from coaching a high school team in Florida, was paid a $200,000 salary. (Fair and Johnson were fired in the wake of the federal investigation, but they were not among the coaches criminally charged. Johnson has been hired as an assistant coach at La Salle University in Philadelphia.) At Kentucky, assistant coach Kenny Payne makes $800,000 a year.

Assistant coaching jobs are hard to get and easy to lose. They are filled by former college players and, increasingly, by coaches who have come out of the grassroots scene and are valued for their recruiting connections. An assistant coach may get into the profession for all the right reasons—teach the game, mentor kids—but if he rises up to one of the top jobs and is making a half million dollars a year, he suddenly finds himself with a lifestyle and mortgage to match his salary. He has grown accustomed to the finer things his salary provides, and so has his family. When the head coach gets fired, the assistants in almost all cases are sent packing. The positions are so coveted that it is difficult to get back into the business, especially at the same level.

People cheat when they have powerful incentives to do so, and many such inducements exist in college basketball. One is the conviction that everyone else is doing it, so it's necessary to break the rules just to keep up. The dirtier a sport or any endeavor becomes, the more rational this belief becomes. Think of international cycling over the last several decades. Who could blame a competitor for thinking he had two choices: cheat in order to survive, or quit the sport. An assistant college basketball coach is not a *domestique*—the term for the riders who serve the lead cyclist on a team, which translates to "servant"—but they are not the Lance Armstrongs of the operation. The head coach is that, and they serve at his pleasure.

Job security—the fear of being fired—is another powerful incentive to cheat. Teachers and school administrators have been caught in recent years manipulating the results of standardized tests, a trend that only began after their raises, career prospects, and sometimes the survival of their schools began to be tied to student performance.

The careers of college basketball coaches rise and fall on the decisions of seventeen- and eighteen-year-olds—and the influences, often hidden, of whoever surrounds those teenagers. "I don't know how the assistant coaches sleep at night," an NBA scout says. "Something happens with a kid you've been on since he was a freshman, or maybe since middle school. He told you he's signing with you, and then all the sudden, he's off in another direction. Did you just waste four years? Is that the end of your job?"

Recruiting requires long days away from home and is labor-intensive and draining. Head coaches at some programs fly on private jets; the assistants, unless they are traveling with their

Rick Pitino in Florida in March 2018. He was exiled from basketball and angry about the FBI investigation and what he viewed as his betrayal at the hands of the University of Louisville.

The hand of Joon H. Kim, then the acting U.S. Attorney for the Southern District of New York, pointing to a chart illustrating the college basketball recruiting case that led to Pitino's downfall.

Brian Bowen Jr., playing for his high school team, La Lumiere School in Indiana, in 2016, shocked the college basketball world by signing to play for Louisville in June 2017. "We got lucky on this one," Pitino said at the time.

Christian Dawkins, a figure on the grassroots basketball circuit, outside the federal courthouse in Lower Manhattan. He was charged with paying bribes to family members of high school players, including the father of Brian Bowen Jr., to induce players to enroll at Adidas-sponsored universities.

Pitino, in 1997, coaching Kentucky in an NCAA tournament game in San Jose, California.

Pitino's teams were known for their fierce competitiveness. Here his 2012 Louisville squad celebrates a come-from-behind victory over Florida in the West Regional in Phoenix that qualified them for the Final Four that season.

A former point guard, Pitino always coached in an athletic stance, with one foot on the court. Here he is exhorting his team in the first half of the 2013 national championship game against Michigan in Atlanta, Georgia.

Pitino takes his turn cutting the net down after his gritty team, with undersized players and just one NBA first-round draft pick, defeated Michigan, 82–76, to win the title.

Karen Cunagin Sypher arrives at the federal courthouse for the second day of her trial in Louisville in July 2010. Pitino admitted to having sex with her after-hours in a closed restaurant. She was convicted of trying to extort money from him in return for staying quiet about the episode and served more than six years in prison.

Katina Powell coauthored a book, *Breaking Cardinal Rules: Basketball and the Escort Queen*, that told of parties at the Louisville basketball dorm over the course of four years involving strippers and sexual favors for players. The scandal became known as Strippergate.

Andre McGee, in action for Louisville against Arizona in a 2009 NCAA tournament game, is a former point guard for Pitino who later served on his staff as director of operations. Powell said in her book that he provided the money for the sex parties in the dormitory.

Sonny Vaccaro, a former promoter of high school basketball all-star games and later an executive with Nike and Adidas, brought the sneaker companies into the college recruiting and grassroots basketball worlds. He said of the current scandal, "Everybody forgot the boundaries of what they could do with their deals."

Former USC assistant Tony Bland, one of four assistant coaches charged by federal prosecutors, on the sideline of a game standing behind head coach Andy Enfield.

Former college and NBA star Chuck Person, another of the assistants charged, stands behind Auburn coach Bruce Pearl and instructs a player during a game.

Tom Jurich, the athletic director who built Louisville into an all-sports powerhouse, walks to a meeting with the university's interim president on the day after news of the recruiting scandal broke. He was dismissed that day.

Pitino and Jurich hold up a sign celebrating Pitino's 700th victory as a college coach after a win in 2014 in Louisville over Cleveland State. He would reach 770 victories, but the official total fell to 647 after the NCAA "vacated" 123 wins as part of the sanctions for the sex parties in the basketball dorm.

bosses, normally do not. Even after a scholarship offer is extended and a player has made a verbal commitment but not yet signed a binding offer, coaches continue to call, text, and show up at games. This is known in the trade as "babysitting"—they don't want some other coach coming in and poaching.

The major grassroots events of the spring and summer are massive affairs, with an annual July event in Las Vegas sponsored by Nike attracting nine hundred teams. Games take place in multiple gyms from nine in the morning until almost midnight. Coaches crisscross the city to check out prospects, and hotel lobbies are thick with players and their families. It's like a giant trade show except that the product is young basketball talent.

Top college teams travel to games with their NCAA "compliance officers," officials in the athletic department who serve almost as bouncers. They keep an eye on the traveling party and make sure that no agents or runners or other unsavory individuals make contact with players. The compliance officers handle the list of complimentary tickets to games and makes sure players are not gifting them to unauthorized individuals.

When a player travels with his high school team, it is likely to be a similarly controlled environment. (Assuming it is an actual high school and not a pop-up basketball academy.) He is with a couple of coaches, at least one of whom may be a teacher at the school.

Las Vegas is nothing like that. Many of the teams stay on the Strip because that's where their coaches want to be. It's summer in Vegas—the rooms are cheap—and besides, the shoe companies have generously funded their travel budgets. "I've got nothing against Vegas. I love Vegas," a veteran coach says. "But think about this whole deal. You've got three thousand players running around the city with AAU coaches as their chaperones."

The setting in Vegas, and at all the other big grassroots events, is ideal for people who want to develop relationships with players and their families. It is known where they are staying, what time the games are, when their downtime is. "You hang in the lobby and wait," says someone familiar with the scene. "You say, 'Hey brother, I know your dad's cousin in Philly. He talks about you all the time. You on Instagram? You on Twitter? Can I DM you?' Or better yet, 'I got tickets for a hip-hop show tonight and I see you guys are done at seven. I could take your family if everybody wants to go?'

"I mean, it's really that easy. Every one of these kids will say they have a tight group around them, but once someone penetrates it and works their way in, they are ripe to be taken advantage of. Think of it as one of those lazy rivers at an amusement park. Somebody jumps in and they're just going around and around with you. Pretty soon, you don't notice them. They're just floating around with you."

The former Big Ten assistant coach says, "When you're recruiting, there's always that one guy, that cloudy figure who's with the family and you can never figure it out. Who is he? Where did he come from? But he's there. And one way or the other, you have to deal with him."

CHAPTER SEVEN

THE SAGINAW CONNECTION

Brian Bowen was considered by most talent evaluators to be a player who would start for a major college program as a freshman. His refined shooting stroke gave him a chance to average double figures in scoring, and he was projected to rebound at a decent rate. He handled the ball well, passed it okay, and defended like most kids coming out of high school: indifferently.

He would help a team but was not what scouts call "special." That's a word they attach to no more than a handful of players every year, and they are specific types: Point guards who combine speed, size, and uncanny court vision and are threats to score themselves or set up teammates for easy hoops. Shooting guards and small forwards with crazy athleticism who can "put their chin on the rim," as it's sometimes said, and can also rain down three-point shots when defenders back off of them. Big men, six foot ten and up, who move with swiftness and grace and can assert themselves near the basket or step outside and shoot from the perimeter. The special players have the potential to take over games for long stretches and to carry teams that make extended runs in the NCAA tournament. They are possible NBA all-stars.

Bowen was good, but he was more of a complementary piece—a second or third scoring option on a team stocked with future pros—than a superstar. "Pitino didn't need Brian Bowen. He would have been fine without him," an NBA scout says. "He's not that special. Maybe he would have become that, but you could say the same about fifty other guys. He's a good shooter, not all that athletic, not a good defender. He wasn't a one-and-done. Maybe a two-and-done."

Tom Konchalski saw Bowen play for MeanStreets, the Nike-sponsored AAU team in Chicago, which he jumped to after leaving Saginaw and his former club, the Adidas-backed Michigan Mustangs. "Did I think he was an NBA player? I don't know about immediately," he said. "But if he had been coached for a year or two by Rick Pitino, he would have been. Few are better at developing kids, really coaching them."

When Bowen finally visited Louisville in the last week of May 2017, he toured the team's 60,000-square-foot, $15 million basketball complex—which includes a two-level weight and cardio center, massage and hydrotherapy areas, an amphitheater with plush leather chairs for film study, and a roomy, wood-paneled locker room with a lounge area and big-screen TVs. At the center of the locker room, inlaid on the floor, was a portion of the basketball court—the center jump circle—from the Georgia Dome on the night Louisville won the 2013 NCAA tournament.

The amenities were the equal of just about any in the NBA, which is de rigueur for top college programs. Much of the money spent at the elite levels of NCAA sports is to keep up appearances and not be outdone by the competition. That's why the facilities are so gilded. It is where the players will all but live, and everything is built to impress. The "arms race" that administrators use as a rationale is a way of saying they have no control over the spending—but what it really amounts to is a competition to lay in expensive stuff that teenage boys will be impressed by.

From his spacious second-floor office, Rick Pitino could step out onto a balcony and look down on his practice court, where hanging against one of the walls were banners commemorating his Final Four appearances in 2005 and 2012 as well as the 2013 national title. A plaque was inscribed with Pitino's "Cardinal Rules." They were largely platitudes about hard work and no excuse making, but one also urged his young players to "treat all women with kindness and respect, just like you would your mother." The walls of Pitino's office and most of the flat surfaces were covered with pictures of his children and grandchildren and all the players from both Louisville and Kentucky whom he had sent on to the NBA.

Bowen had traveled to Louisville with his mother, father, and a man he referred to as a family friend—Christian Dawkins. Just twenty-four years old, and always expensively and impeccably dressed, Dawkins had an air of confidence beyond his years. When they all sat down together in Pitino's office, the coach was already familiar with Dawkins because he was the intermediary who had set Bowen's visit in motion. A week earlier, Dawkins had sent Pitino a text that said, "Coach, this is Christian Dawkins. I dealt with you on Jaylen Johnson. Would you have interest in Brian Bowen or are you done recruiting?"

Jaylen Johnson was from Ypsilanti, Michigan, and played three successful seasons for Pitino, from 2014 to 2017, before passing up his senior year to take a shot at the NBA. (He did not stick for long in the league and was currently playing for the minor-league Windy City Bulls.) His mother, Janetta Johnson, has denied that Dawkins played any role in her son's recruitment.

Pitino had also heard about Bowen from Jim Gatto, the Adidas executive, who called a few days before the campus visit and left Pitino a voice mail. "Coach, Jim Gatto with Adidas. Hope all is well. Sorry to bother you over the weekend, but I just got a call about a player I want to discuss with you," Gatto said, according to a transcript of the voice mail. Pitino knew Gatto but considered it unusual for him to call about a particular player. When they talked on the phone, Gatto told him he could put in a good word with Bowen's family. Pitino, in an interview with the *Washington Post,* said he already had a sense that Bowen was coming his way and thought Gatto was just trying to "take a bow, so to speak." But it's not clear how or why Pitino would have thought that.

Pitino quickly responded to Dawkins's text. "We would love to have him," he wrote.

Pitino has vehemently and repeatedly denied that he had anything to do with—or knew anything about—money changing hands in return for Bowen's decision to attend Louisville.

The meeting between the Bowens and Pitino was in one sense routine, because the coach had been through this same drill hundreds of times at four different college programs, beginning at Boston University in 1978. Bowen, like most high schoolers, wanted to know how he would fit in with the returning players and incoming freshmen and if he had a chance to crack the starting lineup. No player wants to make what at that point is the biggest decision of his life and then find himself with a seat on the bench. Pitino replied as he had to every kid he had recruited over the last four decades—that Bowen had a chance to start if he worked hard, but there were no guarantees. He told him he had great size for a perimeter player and good enough ball-handling ability that he might even be able to play a little point guard in a pinch, but he would have to become a better defensive player. No one came to a Pitino team truly ready for the defensive intensity he demanded. Those who rose to the challenge were rewarded with playing time.

What made the meeting unusual is that Pitino had not seen much of Bowen on the court. Louisville expressed interest early in his high school years, but it was not reciprocated. When Pitino attended AAU events where Bowen was participating, he was more focused on players he seemed to have a realistic chance of signing. In the meeting, he found Bowen quiet and respectful, and his parents seemed pleasant enough. He sold the attributes of the program, as he always did, but the deal seemed to have already weirdly come together. The last five-star in the class of 2017 was coming his way.

Dawkins took an active role in the conversation, and near the end expressed a concern: What about the sanctions still looming over Louisville from the sex parties in the basketball dorm? Would Bowen get a chance to play in the NCAA tournament during his time at Louisville, especially if he stayed just a year or two before bolting for the NBA?

It was a reasonable enough question, though in hindsight the fact that Dawkins was the one asking it seems ironic in the extreme.

O n June 3, 2017, Bowen finally revealed his choice: Louisville and its Hall of Fame coach, Rick Pitino. The *Louisville Courier-Journal* attributed the "surprise twist" to decisions made by players at Arizona, Michigan State, and Texas to stay in school rather than bolt for the NBA and speculated that Bowen did not want to have to compete against established talent for playing time. But players with NBA ambitions and Bowen's pedigree—MVP of the Jordan Brand Classic, a high school team that was ranked the best in the nation, rarely a pickup game he could not dominate— usually figure they will bust their way into any coach's starting lineup. And even if they don't, they can contribute. Coaches almost always give significant playing time to at least two or three players who come off their bench—and it is not that unusual for non-starters to be chosen high in the NBA draft.

The stories gave no real clue about Bowen's timing or motivation, other than that he seemed to be more strategic than most other prospects. In earlier stories, he attributed his delay to there being "a lot more to it" than most people would understand, with so many variables about who might end up on certain rosters. The impression he gave was that he was weighing everything, like a handicapper at the track who keeps his head down in the *Racing Form* until the last possible moment and then finally makes a wager just as the betting window closes.

The announcement sent Louisville fans into ecstasy. Pitino's move to lure a coveted recruit at the last possible moment, and one who did not even have Louisville on his list, was hailed as a masterstroke. Bowen was celebrated as the last piece on a championship team—and a sign that Pitino, as was one of the websites that follows the team put it, was "serious about getting back to the big dance."

Tugs's parents had moved with him to Indiana when he enrolled at La Lumiere—just as they had moved to East Lansing to follow Jason Richardson. They lived only a few miles from Lake Michigan. After he committed to Louisville, the family drove to their favorite spot near the water and took one last photo at sunset.

The next day they set out for Louisville. They took another sunset picture, this one in the park beside the Clark Memorial Bridge, which spans the Ohio River and connects Louisville and Jeffersonville, Indiana. One night they attended an Ed Sheeran concert at the Yum Center. (Tugs had an allergic reaction to something he ate and ended up in the emergency room.)

Some members of their extended family came to visit in Louisville. It was a celebration of Tugs's milestone. He had moved from the basketball court in his Saginaw backyard, up through the grassroots circuit, to MVP of the Jordan Brand Classic, and now onto the roster of the Louisville Cardinals.

When Brian Bowen Sr. and his son walked into the basketball locker room for the first time, Tugs's name and his number 20 were already on one of the big wood-paneled locker stalls. It was not yet mission accomplished, because the NBA was the ultimate goal, but Tugs had fulfilled the first part of the plan. He was at a big-time program and he would be playing on TV just about every week for one of the most famous coaches in America.

To anyone who has spent time around basketball, Christian Dawkins is a recognizable type. He is the kid who has no game but wants to be involved, so he figures out another way into the action. He knows the good players and can talk to them about their best moves, about some fool they made look bad in a recent game, and some other hotshot on the circuit who thinks too highly of himself. He stokes egos and promotes rivalries—*You believe he's talkin' that shit about you?*—and serves the purpose of making everything seem bigger. He has the scouting report on the next game, a ride there if you need one, and entry to the party that night.

On the day of the meeting in Pitino's office, he was immersed in the business of basketball recruiting in two different ways: as a matchmaker between high school players and college coaches, and as a runner, or go-between, for agents and financial advisors seeking to sign up players with NBA potential. It is one business, really, because in the one-and-done era, the best players choose a college, play their 30-some NCAA games, and are sitting in the greenroom of the NBA draft, all within a span of about twelve months.

Dawkins could get it all wired on the front end: Negotiate with the college program on behalf of a player, and, for the best ones, get payments into the six figures. Establish the shoe company affiliation. And have the financial team in place for when the kid is ready to jump to the NBA.

He had no college education, but Dawkins could carry himself like he had been through law school. He spoke the language of the boardroom as well as the street. He was, of course, a walking, talking violator of NCAA regulations and a dispenser of "impermissible benefits," but he dwelled in a realm in which the rules were not followed and not respected as having any moral authority. Not by the recruits themselves. And not by their families, their AAU coaches, or many of the NCAA coaches seeking their services.

The indefensible nature of the NCAA itself, a multibillion-dollar enterprise resting on a pool of unpaid labor, created a gray market and an opportunity for under-the-table deal-making. And it gave power to—and put money in the pockets of—practitioners like Christian Dawkins.

His employer at that time was Andy Miller, a top NBA agent who over the years represented dozens of players, from now-retired stars Kevin Garnett and Chauncey Billups to current Knicks forward Kristaps Porzingis. Dawkins had previously been a recruiter for a firm of financial advisors who represented NBA players, but left that job in rancor and litigation, including an allegation that he somehow ran up $42,000 in Uber bills on the credit card of an NBA player. That's a lot of rides, but it also gives a sense of Dawkins's energy and style—constantly in motion and always working.

Agents, especially the older and more settled ones, need runners who can melt into the grassroots scene. Even if the agents were once good at it themselves, they are less likely as the years go on to want to work the sidelines at tournaments and the hotel lobbies at night. White agents are particularly in need of young, African American operatives like Dawkins in what is largely a milieu of black players and their families. Dawkins referred to the young men he had brought to Miller as "my players," though they were not technically that since he was not a registered NBA agent.

He did not have to go far to find Brian Bowen Jr., because they grew up within a couple of miles of each other and their families were close. Even though he was not much of a player himself, Christian Dawkins came from Saginaw basketball royalty. His father, Lou, was a legendary high school player in the city who went on to play at Tulsa University, where he hit a shot that is still considered the highest moment in his alma mater's basketball history—a last-second three-pointer that put Tulsa into the Sweet 16 of the 1994 NCAA tournament. It was the first NCAA tournament for his coach, Tubby Smith, who would go on to win an NCAA title at Kentucky.

Lou Dawkins hoped for an NBA career, but when no NBA team drafted him, he returned home and went to work as a teacher and coach at Saginaw High, first paying his dues by working six years as the junior varsity coach. In seven seasons as the varsity coach, he won two state championships and coached eleven players who went on to play Division I basketball. His teams were ranked as high as second in the nation, and he won a couple of Michigan coach of the year honors. When he moved on in 2013 for a job in college coaching—he is now an assistant at Cleveland State—one of his former players who attended the press conference in Saginaw was NBA all-star Draymond Green, who referred to Lou Dawkins as his "teacher, mentor, and father figure."

Looking at Christian Dawkins through the prism of his family and their accomplishments, it is possible to view him as both an underachiever and an overachiever. His father, in addition to his coaching role at Saginaw, was a teacher and the school's athletic director. His mother is a high school principal. Christian took a few classes at Kishwaukee College, a two-year school in DeKalb County, Illinois, before dropping out. And yet he traveled the nation and world, sat courtside at NBA games, and mixed with multimillion-aire athletes. He had the private numbers of NBA general managers in his phone—his *phones,* actually, as he had three of them—and when he called, they picked up.

His social media posts celebrated this dazzling existence: On his Facebook page is a screen grab of him on ESPN during the 2017 NBA draft at the Barclays Center in Brooklyn. From a fancy-looking hotel pool, a selfie is captioned, "View from the corner office this morning." A close-up of a lobster on a plate at a restaurant in Sint Maarten is tagged, "This is a long way from Red Lobster, slim."

One of the comments on that post was, "Naw, Cuz, that's a long way frm Saginaw #proudofyouyoungmn." That seemed to be a goal of Dawkins—to be, or at least appear to be, a long way from Saginaw even while remaining immersed in its basketball culture.

D awkins had a younger brother, Dorian, who was a gifted player like their dad, perhaps even better. The stories of his exploits make him seem like a young Paul Bunyan of the hoops world. By the sixth grade, he was the first one chosen in any pickup game, even when the other players included members of Saginaw High's varsity team. In the first game of his eighth-grade season, he had 36 points, 20 assists, and 22 steals—and it would have been an even more impressive stat line if he had not sat out the fourth quarter because his team was so far out in front. He was known as "The Future" from just about the first moment he first touched a basketball.

Off the court, Dorian shared his brother Christian's ability to connect with people. "He had a rich personality, above average amount of confidence for a kid that age, and incredible versatility in terms of using it," Curtis Hervey, one of his former coaches, told the *Lansing State Journal* after his death. "In sports, in class, in dealing with nonathletes, across racial lines, he was just a really smooth guy to be that young."

Dorian just naturally drew both kids and adults into his circle. In grade school, his parents would sometimes go to pick him up at the end of the day but have to wait because he was locked in a chess match with the principal.

Christian spoke of his brother's physical courage. "There would be stuff I was scared of, he wouldn't be scared of. Say you were around the neighborhood and somebody would do something like steal your bike or take your next game in basketball. I'd think, 'I don't want to fight that dude.' He'd say, 'Let's just fight them and get it back.'"

In the summer of 2009, Dorian was fourteen years old and playing in a grassroots tournament on the campus of Michigan State for his father's AAU team. Lou Dawkins had another commitment and the team was being led by his assistant coach. Christian, two years older than his brother, was also along on the trip. Late in a game, Dorian stepped to the foul line and made a shot that tied the game—and then collapsed on the court. Christian rode in an ambulance with him to the hospital. "He just said that he was hurting, and he didn't know what was going on and just to call Momma and Daddy," Christian recalled. His parents sped the hundred miles from Saginaw to East Lansing, but Dorian died before they reached him. An autopsy revealed that he had a congenital heart defect and had suffered a series of heart attacks that day.

Dorian was ranked among the top incoming ninth graders in the country, and the tournament, called the Tom Izzo Shootout, was one of the summer's big AAU events. Michigan State coach Izzo spent much of that night with the Dawkins family and released a statement. "As a coach and even more so as a parent, I grieve, pray, and suffer with the Dawkins family, and the many people in Saginaw and beyond who mourn the passing of a wonderful young man."

Lou Dawkins would later say, "When he died, I died." When he and his wife left Saginaw a few years later and Lou took his first college job, as an assistant at Northern Illinois, he said the move was as much to get away from the memories as it was to chase a career goal.

A s his brother was establishing himself on the court, Christian Dawkins was laying the foundation for his own future in the game. By his mid-teens, he was publishing a recruiting newsletter, *Best of the Best Prep Basketball Scouting,* that charged $40 a subscription. Few people paying for it realized it was the work of a fifteen-year-old. He formed a company called Living Out Your Dreams Enterprises.

He made his father's high school team, but he was a bench player—about six feet tall, with a soft physique and not much in the way of skills or grit. But he ranked himself the third best player in the state of Michigan in his own recruiting sheet. His self-rating won him a tryout with one of the top AAU teams in the Boston area, the New England Playaz, which paid for his airfare. They took a one-day look at him and realized they'd been tricked.

The tryout coincided with Dawkins's transfer to St. Mark's School, a tony prep school in Southborough, Massachusetts, west of Boston. He told people he was recruited to play basketball, but the coaches there were no more impressed by his talent than the New England Playaz had been. He seemed to like talking about basketball—arguing about the relative merits of players he watched on TV—more than actually playing.

Dawkins struggled academically in his freshman year at St. Mark's and might not have returned anyway, but when his brother died that summer, he transferred back to Saginaw. He also took over his father's AAU program. He had heard somewhere that a person "never dies unless they are forgotten," so he renamed the team Dorian's Pride. He began running tournaments for the best local AAU teams and all-star events that drew players from a wider area. One was called the Showdown in the Valley, another the Show Your Heart Memorial Classic.

His events became important destinations on the grassroots circuit, and he was able to attract top players and sponsorship money from three different shoe companies. He started getting some press as well. The website MaxPreps, in a 2010 profile, surveyed the breadth of his basketball involvement and observed, "Not a bad resume for a 17-year-old."

The tournaments served as business development. Dawkins was gaining access to people from every level of the industry—from young players and their families to scouts, agents, pro and college coaches, and all the way up to NBA general managers. "There are a lot of Dawkins figures out there, but they're not as persistent and aggressive as he was," says an NBA scout who has been dealing with Dawkins since he was a teenager. "It's a job like any other job, but he worked really hard at it and he thought really hard at it. He was on kids before other people were, and by the time anyone else showed up at their front door, he had them signed, sealed, and delivered.

"The sad thing is he had good intentions in the beginning. He genuinely loves basketball. He wanted to honor his brother and I think he wanted to do good things. But he got so big in such a short amount of time, bigger than someone his age and with his experience should ever have been."

By the time he graduated from high school, Dawkins was so deeply immersed in the grassroots culture, and so familiar with its customs, byways, and dark corners, that college was not of great interest. He made a halfhearted stab at it, then tried to raise money to start his own agency, promising prospective investors that he could immediately deliver clients. Even for someone as self-confident as Dawkins, that was too audacious, and he was not successful in setting up his own shop. He continued to run tournaments as he established himself as a broker in recruiting—someone who could navigate an unfamiliar landscape for high school recruits and their families, speak the local language, and get the best possible deal. At the same time, he introduced NBA agents and financial advisors to the players he had befriended, so he could have skin in the game when his recruits left college.

In April 2014, Dawkins was hired by International Management Advisors, a Cleveland-based firm with a clientele of NBA players. It was headed by Kurt Schloeppler, LeBron James's former financial advisor. Dawkins became the firm's "executive director of sports and entertainment." He was twenty-one years old.

Despite the lofty title, Dawkins was what anyone in the industry would recognize as a runner. He recruited clients. It was what he had been doing; now he was just working for someone else. In documents related to litigation after Dawkins was dismissed a year into the job, IMA defined his role as "developing relationships with future NBA players such that the players would select IMA to serve as their agent and/or financial advisor during and after their NBA playing career." It made clear that his hunting grounds were to be college campuses, among supposedly amateur athletes who by NCAA rules are prohibited from signing with agents or accepting any benefits from them.

After Dawkins left IMA, he went to work for Andy Miller, the NBA agent. IMA's civil action, which has since been settled, alleged that Dawkins was two-timing IMA—steering prospects to Miller while he was on the road at their expense. (Miller was the defendant in the suit.) "By January 2015, it became apparent that Dawkins was actually representing [Miller's] interests, not IMA's, when interacting with prospects, and he could no longer be trusted as the Executive Director of Sports and Entertainment," the complaint said. IMA was also seeking reimbursement of the $42,722 of Uber fares allegedly charged by Dawkins while using an American Express card belonging to one of its clients, NBA guard Elfrid Payton.

Recruiting is the lifeblood of agents, just as it is for college coaches. NBA agents generally take commissions of 4 percent of playing contracts. Rookie contracts, which last for either two or three years, are "slotted," meaning they are set by a player's draft position, so an agent does not have to do much negotiating. The dollars are already determined. Basketball agents maintain that their connections with NBA general managers and expertise at marketing players to teams enhance their clients' draft positions, and therefore the size of their contracts.

Competition for clients is rugged, and Dawkins's new employer, Andy Miller, had already been penalized for playing outside the rules. In 2002, a jury ordered Miller to pay another agent, Eric Fleisher, $4.6 million, after Fleisher accused him of improperly poaching sixteen clients, including Garnett and Chauncey Billups. (Miller appealed, and the two agents ended up settling for an undisclosed sum.)

Eight years later an arbitrator ordered Miller to pay $40,000 in damages to another agent whose client he had taken, allegedly by working in concert with the player's high school coach. The financial penalty was modest, but as a law professor, Gabriel Feldman, director of Tulane's sports law program, noted in a *New York Times* story, "It's rare for an agent to successfully sue another agent for client-poaching, or tampering, or tortious interference, or whatever you want to call it." Miller had now lost two such suits.

Miller had represented twenty-six first-round draft choices and negotiated more than $1 billion in contracts. But after the retirement of Garnett and some of his other high-paid properties, his business was perceived to be, if not in decline, then not quite as booming as it once had been. He had endured all manner of challenges in his nearly quarter century in the business, including the contempt of many of his fellow agents. But what Miller ultimately could not survive was the young man from Saginaw he hired to help find him new clients.

T he FBI's probe of college basketball began by happenstance, which is not unusual. Law enforcement agents often start off in one direction, with a single suspect and a discrete set of facts, and then are led to something else—a bigger case or sometimes just a more interesting one. In this instance, they were initially looking into the business practices of Louis Martin Blazer III, known as Marty, a Pittsburgh financial advisor with a client list of professional athletes. His company, Blazer Capital, touted itself as a "concierge" firm that in addition to investment guidance took care of clients' bill-paying, developed and managed their personal budgets, and assisted in tax preparation.

Blazer had a side interest in moviemaking, and in 2010 he began to raise money for two films, one of which was named *Mafia, the Movie*. He created a financial instrument related to its funding, "Mafia LLC" (a name that seems preordained to attract interest from law enforcement), but struggled to find backers.

The Securities and Exchange Commission filed a civil case against him, alleging, "To compensate for the shortfall, Blazer simply took funds from client accounts over which he had control and used the money to finance the films." When one client protested about the unauthorized use of $550,000 and threatened legal action, Blazer, who had previously worked at Smith Barney and Merrill Lynch, returned the client's money and took the same amount from a different client, according to the SEC complaint. The government referred to Blazer's shuffling of funds as "Ponzi-like payments."

This, of course, is the type of activity that, once discovered, puts an individual in serious legal jeopardy. Criminal charges followed the civil action lodged by the SEC. As a way of mitigating his peril and lessening the potential penalties and jail time, Blazer told federal agents that he could bring them a new case—evidence of criminal behavior in the world of college basketball recruiting. He turned state's evidence and began operating as an undercover agent. "He was inserted," the acting U.S. attorney at the time, Joon Kim, explained on the day the NCAA case was announced. In the documents filed by the U.S. Department of Justice, Blazer is referred to as "CW-1"—cooperating witness number one.

Under the direction of federal agents, Blazer secretly made audio and video recordings of his meetings with college coaches, players, and others in the college basketball universe. His phone conversations with them were recorded. He would eventually team up with an unsuspecting Dawkins, but the first person he pulled into his web was Rashan Michel, a singularly colorful figure—a former NBA referee turned bespoke tailor to players and coaches.

A whole industry has grown up around the needs of lavishly paid professional athletes. Agents and financial advisors, of course.

Assistants (often family members) who live with them and attend to day-to-day household management. Nutritionists and physical trainers. Moving consultants who specialize in quickly relocating them when they are abruptly traded and find them homes in their new cities and even private schools for their children.

Michel officiated his first NBA game in 1995, at twenty-one years old, after the league locked out its regular referees in a labor dispute. He was hired full time in 1997 but let go four years later because his performance put him near the bottom of the league's rankings of its officials. (He continued to officiate men's and women's NCAA games as recently as the 2016–17 season.) After he lost his NBA job, he became a salesman for high-end menswear, and then went through an intensive six-month tailoring course in Toronto. He set up shop in Atlanta and made suits for NBA and NFL players as well as for coaches—in particular, college basketball coaches. In 2016, he traveled to the Final Four in Houston, where he offered "bespoke garment packages" that included a deal for four suits, four shirts, and four ties for $4,000.

Michel claimed to have outfitted the first seven picks in the 2014 NFL draft. A writer for *HuffPost* spent the day with him as he received players in his hotel suite, tending to last-minute refinements in their ensembles, and produced a breathless account. "Sprawled on the bed were tailored made shirts with each of Rashan's clients' initials embedded on the sleeves alongside a multitude of socks, ties and men accessories," wrote Marjoriet T. Matute. "Along the counter were jewels and sparkling diamonds lined up to perfection as you would find in a fine showcase. Accompanying the array of designer clothing were ladies luxuries for those lucky women escorting the nation's top picks to the prestigious Radio City Music Hall." An associate of his said, "We are creating a complete turn-key experience and concierge service dressing them from head to toe."

Michel had made news of a different kind three years earlier when he got into a fistfight courtside at an Atlanta Hawks game with retired NBA Hall of Famer Dominique Wilkins. The beef was over money he believed Wilkins owed him for tailoring. (He had previously tweeted at Wilkins, "Pay your debts, poser.") He was arrested—Michel's mug shot from the city lockup shows him with a shiner and a big lump under his left eye, indicating he got the worst of the fracas—but the charges were dropped, and he sued Wilkins for damages. (The case was settled out of court.)

Marty Blazer knew Rashan Michel through a common friend, a sports agent, according to the criminal complaint. Michel, unaware that Blazer was secretly working with the FBI, offered to set him up with college coaches who would accept bribes in return for bringing their players to his financial services firm. In a conversation recorded by the government, he says, "The good thing about it is, I got all the college coaches right now because guess what, I'm the one that's with them. . . . I make all their suits."

He added that he had access to the locker room and the players and said, "The fucking basketball guys [get] way more money than these fucking football guys. . . . We can get us goddamn ten basketball players in the next five years and we [just] sit back and do absolutely nothing."

The two of them allegedly entered into a scheme with Chuck Person, an assistant coach at Auburn who had played there in the early 1980s. A teammate of Charles Barkley's at Auburn, Person was such a dead-eye shooter he was nicknamed "The Rifleman." He went on to play for fourteen NBA seasons, then served as an assistant coach in the league before being hired on to Auburn head coach Bruce Pearl's staff in 2014. Like the other assistant coaches charged in the federal case, Person was making good money, an annual salary of $240,000. His pro career ended in 2001, when NBA players were not compensated as highly as now, but he still made close to $23 million in his playing career.

A theme of the government's case was the willingness of adults—coaches and others—to leverage their relationships with young players, many of them still in their teens, for personal gain. According to prosecutors, after Michel and Blazer met with Person at a restaurant in Alabama, he agreed to "steer" players to them in return for a $60,000 loan. For every player who agreed to do business with them—to buy suits from Michel and use the financial services of Blazer—some of the loan would be forgiven. Michel allegedly tried to extract additional payments from Blazer in exchange for introducing him to "additional coaches who wished to receive bribe payments."

In December 2016, Auburn traveled to New York to play Boston College in a shoe-company-sponsored event called the Under Armour Reunion. They lost the game, 72–71, when an opposing player tipped the ball in with two-tenths of a second left on the clock. In a Manhattan hotel room before the game, Person brought one of his players, whom he considered a surefire NBA prospect, to meet Blazer and Michel—a meeting captured on tape by the FBI. The government's charging documents quote Person as offering what sounds almost like fatherly advice to his player: "This is how the NBA players get it done, they get early relationships, and they form partnerships, they form trust, you get to know Blazer, you get to know Rashan, a lot like Rashan can get you suits and stuff. . . . You'll start looking like an NBA player, that's what you are." He continued, "Don't flaunt the stuff you get, and you know, don't change the way you speak to people, that's very important, too . . . and character . . . which we talk about all the time."

After the meeting, according to the government, and outside the player's presence, Blazer gave Person $15,000 in a briefcase— money that had been supplied by the FBI.

The indictment states that Person, before urging his player into a business relationship with Blazer, never asked about Blazer's qualifications, his client base, or his history of successfully managing money. It also notes dryly that by May 2016, a "simple Internet search" of Blazer's name would have revealed that he was in hot water with the SEC for alleged securities fraud.

In other words, the FBI sent a cooperating witness on the road— operating under his own name—whom anyone could have figured out was someone they should not do business with (legitimate business *or* shady business). The government made a calculation that their targets were not cautious or smart enough to just Google the name "Marty Blazer"—and they were right.

When Joon Kim, then the acting U.S. attorney for the Southern District of New York, stepped up to a podium in September 2017 and dropped his bombshell of a sports story—revealing for the first time that the FBI had been running a two-year probe of NCAA basketball—he decried coaches who "betrayed the trust of their players" and all those who dwelled in the game's "dark underbelly" and saw kids as business investments. Managers and financial advisors, he said, "were circling blue-chip prospects like coyotes."

The probe had been "covert," he said, and even though it was now out in the open, it was ongoing. He urged those who knew about corruption in college basketball to come forward and anyone guilty of it themselves to turn themselves in. "It's better for you to be calling us," he said, "than us to be calling you when we're ready to charge you."

The behaviors described by Kim were cynical and disturbing, but for those versed in the sport, not exactly surprising. Much more shocking was the involvement of federal law enforcement in a realm that previously had been policed, however haphazardly, by the NCAA. If Kim's words were to be taken at face value, he seemed to betray some naïveté when he said that he hoped the charges would "help keep the sport clean and honest." No one involved in college basketball would say the game had been clean or honest in their lifetime.

On the morning of the press conference, FBI agents had already been out on the streets for hours. They arrested ten people charged in the investigation and booked them at the closest federal court-house. Later that day, they reportedly raided the North Jersey offices of Andy Miller, seized documents, and confiscated his computer. He has not been charged, but after two decades as a top-tier agent, he relinquished his certification from the NBA Players Association, and the union announced that he "was no longer permitted to represent players in contract negotiations."

It is important to understand that most of the suspects were not considered by their peers to be especially bad actors. They were mainstream, well known, and well liked. They were part of the basketball fraternity.

College basketball coaching is a sales job—you sell yourself, the program, its record of sending players into the NBA—and Joon Kim and the FBI collared some of the game's best salesmen. The coaches he charged shared personality traits with Christian Dawkins: They were extroverts and relentless networkers. They were bullshitters, when the moment called for that particular talent.

Emanuel Richardson, forty-four, an assistant coach at Arizona known as "Book" (a nickname from childhood because he liked to rummage in his grandmother's pocketbook), was a basketball lifer who had parlayed a mediocre playing career and superior interpersonal skills into ever better and more lucrative jobs. The criminal complaint quotes him as telling one of his alleged co-conspirators that he took pride in being "a people's guy, a relationship guy."

After playing high school basketball in New York and college ball for three different middling programs, he began coaching with the New York Gauchos, one of the nation's premier AAU programs, before landing college assistant jobs at Marist, Xavier, and Arizona. A feature story on Richardson described his trademarks as "A hug. A backslap. An extended handshake. A fist bump. Love, in whatever form." Sean Miller, Arizona's head coach and his former boss at Xavier, counted on Richardson to recruit back east, and especially in New York, where he retained his hometown connections.

The *Los Angeles Times* wrote about Tony Bland, another of the defendants, an assistant coach at the University of Southern California before he was fired in the wake of the federal charges, back when he was a junior at L.A.'s Westchester High and a star for a prominent Nike-sponsored AAU team. It was 1997, and the newspaper even then was looking into relationships between the shoe companies and grassroots basketball programs. Bland was personable but, perhaps owing to his youth, unguarded. "If you need something, you just ask," he told the reporter. "Shoes, shirts, jerseys, hats, socks, you name it. I've got shoes still in boxes."

The paper quoted several people who observed Bland in action as a USC assistant. "There are a lot of guys who can do X's and O's, but there aren't a lot of guys who can go into Westchester or Compton or Harvard-Westlake and immediately have a connection with a coach or his AAU coach or know someone his parents played with," said a journalist who covered AAU basketball in San Diego.

Bland was a connector who could relate to all people at all levels of the game, from young kids on the grassroots circuit up to their fathers and grandfathers. "You go to basketball games and big high school tournaments, Tony knows every kid that's in the gym," Pat Roy, the coach at Inglewood High, said. "Every kid wants to come over and shake his hand."

Jim Gatto had an important-sounding title at Adidas. When Kim announced the charges, he said three of the ten defendants were from a major international sporting goods company, "including its global marketing director for basketball."

In reality, Gatto was just another denizen of the grassroots world and a regular on the sidelines at tournaments. The son of a high school basketball coach in Queens, he went to work for Adidas a year after graduating from tiny Elmira College in upstate New York, and after twenty-five years with the company, he was making $139,000 a year. He lived in Portland with his wife, a sales associate at Ann Taylor, their two children, and a white Lab named Coach.

Konchalski, the seventy-two-year-old scouting guru, had coached Gatto at a summer basketball camp when he was a teenager and had long been friends with his father. He dutifully attended

Gatto's court appearances to lend support. "He's a person you would be proud to have as a son," he said. "He's a very nice person. They came in early in the morning to arrest him and led him away in handcuffs in front of his children. Why was that necessary? If he's guilty of something, it's because he's part of a corrupt system."

CHAPTER EIGHT

THE PLAYBOOK

I f you accept that college basketball is both a sport and a swamp, a coast-to-coast lowland populated by confidence men offering bribes (and not very big ones, by the way, since it does not take much to influence young players and their families), then what Book Richardson, Tony Bland, and Jim Gatto had in common was bad luck. They may not have been engaging in conduct outside the norms of their industry, but they associated with the wrong guy at the wrong time. The same could be said of Rick Pitino and the formerly blue-chip basketball program at the University of Louisville. Terrible luck.

After Christian Dawkins was arrested, his lawyer, Steve Haney, said, "He's not an agent, first of all. He is being represented as being this high-powered basketball agent out of Atlanta, Georgia. He's never been an agent. He doesn't even have a college degree. He couldn't qualify to be an agent. He's twenty-four years old. He lives with his mom and dad."

Although Dawkins did have his own apartment in Atlanta and spent time there, the essence of what Haney said was indisputable. By traditional measures, his client was a small-time hustler. But Dawkins's peripatetic existence, his three iPhones, his ambition and energy, his habit of firing off emails that memorialized everywhere he had been and everyone he had talked to, served to infect and possibly incriminate a wide swath of the recruiting and coaching worlds. Dawkins was not working for the FBI and he was not an undercover agent—or a cooperating witness, like Marty Blazer— but if he *had* been working in concert with federal law enforcement, he could not possibly have done a better job for them.

When the charges were announced, it was William Sweeney Jr., assistant director of the FBI's New York office, who made the statement that sent a wave of paranoia through the ranks of college basketball—"We have your playbook." They obtained it, largely, through Dawkins.

There are 351 Division I basketball programs, but a much smaller number that compete for the best prospects. Dawkins knew all the coaches at those schools. He knew the kids on the radar of the top programs and their families. In fact, he had closer relationships inside the homes than most of the coaches doing the recruiting. He knew the fringe figures, including Rashan Michel. (He had bought suits from Michel and liked the quality, but complained that if you ordered just one, he would send you four and expect you to pay.) He moved from one person to the next, meeting whoever it seemed to him could advance his business goals.

He met Marty Blazer, the Pittsburgh financial advisor, in the spring of 2015. The person who introduced them was Michel. Dawkins began working with Blazer, not knowing of course that Blazer had already been flipped by law enforcement and "inserted" into the recruiting world. Dawkins at this point was employed by the NBA agent Andy Miller and trying to sign clients for him. In early 2017, Dawkins would separate from Miller. Documents filed by federal prosecutors say he was fired; his lawyer, Haney, has said the split was amicable and he continued to do some work with Miller. Either way, Dawkins had long been out in the field, working for Miller and still also hoping to establish his own firm. He always had his eye on the next thing.

The first meeting documented by the FBI between Dawkins and a college assistant coach was in March 2016, with Lamont Evans, who was then at the University of South Carolina. Like Book Richardson and Tony Bland, Evans had been a journeyman player; he competed for two small colleges before landing a scholarship at Division I Drake, then set off on an odyssey that took him to professional teams in Slovenia, Germany, Finland, and Venezuela. But he paid his dues and moved up in the coaching profession. He would move on from South Carolina in 2017 to take an assistant coaching job at Oklahoma State, signing a three-year, $1.85 million contract.

At a restaurant near South Carolina's campus in Columbia, Dawkins met with Evans and Blazer, along with a third man, Munish Sood—a financial advisor in Princeton, New Jersey. Dawkins wanted to set up a financial management firm for athletes with Blazer, and Sood was to be their partner. Dawkins took on the role of instructor, telling his colleagues why it was so important for them to engage coaches like Evans, who serve as gatekeepers to the players, and not just to work though the agents who negotiate playing contracts. As in so many other settings, he was inadvertently giving the feds the playbook.

"Agents obviously have influence, but you gotta get the college coaches, too," he said, because "it's almost like skipping a step if you just deal with agents." They were discussing a particular player at South Carolina, but Dawkins said that signing him would lead to "five players down the line." He advised them to "get in bed" with Evans "so now you got complete access to a kid because if the coach says nobody can come around—can't nobody fucking come around."

Dawkins continued with the tutorial. He said the path to securing commitments from college players goes through the assistants because the head coaches "ain't willing to [take bribes] 'cause they're making too much money and it's too risky." Sood agreed. "In this business," he said, "all you have is trust."

They agreed to pay Evans $2,000 a month, and also to make separate payments that Evans would forward to high school players he was recruiting. At another meeting, Evans spoke of a player he was about to introduce them to as "the motherfucker that's scoring 22 points a game. . . . NBA people are coming to see him, and I'm getting feedback. He's a pro." The whole idea was that Dawkins and company would manage the future earnings of players like him.

Christian Dawkins had meetings in restaurants, in hotel rooms, on a boat docked off Manhattan. The FBI tracked him from state to state, location to location. They were granted court-ordered wiretaps of his phones and listened in on his conversations, and when he made new relationships with coaches and others, they tapped the phones of some of those people, too. He was a young man who did a lot of boasting, but that did not seem to bother the people he did business with or make them wary. He had been in the business for years and they granted him his authority.

The federal documents say that Dawkins enlisted an Adidas consultant, Merl Code, forty-three, into his schemes. Code played point guard for Clemson in the 1990s and came from an outstanding family. He is the grandson of a high school principal and the son of a retired judge and prominent community leader in Greenville, South Carolina, who established a lifetime of firsts—first African American to serve as a municipal judge in his city, first to serve as chairman of the local Chamber of Commerce, first to serve as chairman of the United Way. The younger Code was a respected athlete and student at Clemson, and when he was arrested, a post on one of the university's sports blogs asked, "Is this our Merl Code?"

When the government set out to explore possible criminality in college basketball, it had Blazer as an asset, the investment advisor charged with financial fraud who had been turned into a government informant. They gave him a fictional partner, an undercover FBI agent who posed as someone who could supply the operation with money. (He did, at times—FBI money.) As the probe widened, at least one other undercover agent joined the mix. At trial, there are likely to be a number of cooperating witnesses called by the prosecution, including, it is likely, assistant coaches and other basketball insiders who have avoided prosecution by agreeing to help the government.

The government's charges portray Code as a willing partner of Dawkins. At a meeting on June 20, 2017, he met with Dawkins, Blazer, and the undercover agent posing as Blazer's business associate at a Manhattan hotel, where Code agreed to identify coaches "who would be willing to accept bribe payments." At the end of the meeting, the government says, the undercover agent gave Code $5,000 in cash.

A few weeks later, the FBI listened in on a phone conversation between Code and Dawkins. They were discussing an upcoming trip to a big grassroots tournament, which, like all such events, would attract the coaching staffs at the top programs. Code told Dawkins that he could introduce him to a number of coaches, and said he expected $5,000 for each introduction.

Dawkins met with Tony Bland, the USC coach, at a hotel room in Las Vegas—a meeting the FBI says was arranged by Code and also attended by Blazer and the undercover agent. Bland was more cautious than some of the others. He said he did not want to "touch" the money intended to go to his current players or ones he was re- cruiting, but would arrange meetings where Dawkins and his co- horts could deliver it directly. "I can definitely mold the players and put them in the lap of you guys," Bland said, adding that he was in accord with how they were suggesting things should be done, "par- ticularly because it comes from Christian, who I trust."

Through most of the time the FBI listened in, Dawkins was try- ing to raise money from Blazer and his "business associates," undercover agents, to fund his management company. To in- crease the amount they were willing to contribute, he stressed the status of the coaches and college programs he had compromised. If Dawkins and his cohorts were going to manage the money of pro basketball players, the major college teams were the source of the biggest piles of it. They had the greatest number of future NBA players, the potential all-stars, and the plumpest potential earnings.

Exhibit A in his effort to demonstrate his access to these premier programs was Emanuel "Book" Richardson, the Arizona assistant coach. The Wildcats had long since supplanted UCLA as the perennial college basketball power in the West. Under former coach Lute Olson, Arizona reached the Final Four of the NCAA tournament four times between 1988 and 2002, including a national title in 1997; his successor, Sean Miller, hired in 2009, led the team into the tourney in seven of his first eight seasons and three times reached the Elite Eight. The 2017 opening-night rosters in the NBA included thirteen Arizona players, ten of them first-round draft choices—including nine who were among the first ten players selected.

Sean Miller did not yet have the NCAA tournament résumé of Rick Pitino, but with the help of Book Richardson and his other recruiters, he had far surpassed him in his ability to produce players picked near the top of the NBA draft. "I can go to Arizona's practices like I'm on the team," Dawkins said in an intercepted telephone conversation. Referring to the Arizona's coaches, he added, "We're all friends."

In another phone conversation, he told Richardson he should ask for $5,000 or more a month, since he could provide such high-end talent, and "do whatever the fuck you want to do with the money." He said he could use it to help in recruiting, "or fucking just go on vacation with it."

The documents describe a meeting in a hotel room in New York, attended by Dawkins, Richardson, and Sood, as well as Blazer and an undercover agent, both of whom were wearing recording devices. Richardson laid out what his approach would be in binding his players to the new management firm, explaining that he used to give players three or four options, but now realized that was not advisable because "they look like men, but they're kids." To put too many options in front of them, he said, was like "putting a Band-Aid over a bullet hole."

Before he left the meeting, Richardson accepted $5,000 in an envelope from the undercover agent, the government alleges. It was allegedly payment for his future services—his ability to deliver his players to Dawkins and his cohorts.

Later, Dawkins followed up with a call to the undercover agent to tell him Richardson might be needing more money in order to land a coveted recruiting target, one of the top high school point guards in the nation. The head coach, he explained, wanted the kid "bad as fuck. So, I mean, the leverage I have with the program would be ridiculous at that point." The federal case portrays Dawkins as someone who has a strategy in building his business. He assembles assets—the players and coaches—and one leads to the next. But they are not all equal. Some give him more credibility and add juice to the whole enterprise.

At a meeting on a boat docked off Manhattan in June 2017, Dawkins touted the value of Book Richardson relative to some of the other coaches they had lured. "Lamont's good but he's not one of the elite, elite dudes," he said, referring to Oklahoma State's Lamont Evans. "I love Lamont to death but he don't have the resources."

Richardson and other coaches at his level, he said, promised a much bigger return. Arizona was a recruiting dynamo, just about on par with Duke, Kentucky, and Kansas. If they kept Richardson happy, he could provide access to a steady stream of NBA lottery picks. "If you're gonna fund those kind of guys, man, I mean, like we'd be running college basketball," Dawkins said.

On a drizzly gray morning in February 2018, defense lawyers in the case trudged into a courtroom on the twenty-first floor of the Daniel Patrick Moynihan federal courthouse in lower Manhattan. The proceeding was a pretrial hearing to hear motions filed by the defense. Presiding was Judge Lewis Kaplan, a seventy-three-year-old jurist and Harvard Law School graduate who over the last quarter century had heard numerous big cases, including the only criminal prosecution in federal court of a Guantánamo detainee. Forbearance in the course of argumentation he found unworthy did not appear to be one of the judge's strengths.

The defendants were charged with a range of offenses, including fraud, bribery, and conspiracy. Their attorneys were likely to stipulate to most of the facts in the government's case. They didn't have a choice. Their clients were on tape. They were on camera in the meetings. It was hard to argue with. The defense lawyers would instead focus on legal arguments, and one in particular: A criminal charge of fraud, under federal law, must have an identifiable victim. But who were the victims in this case? Who was hurt by the schemes?

The government identified the universities as the victims, arguing that they were defrauded because Dawkins and others caused them to unknowingly enroll players whom they knew, under NCAA rules, would be ineligible. By playing them, the universities could have their reputations sullied and suffer economic harm—including the possible revocation of TV revenue and other money paid out by the NCAA for their participation in the annual tournament. The defense, however, contended that the defendants were not defrauding the purported victims but, rather, assisting them by helping them get the players they wanted. They may have done so by unsavory methods, but who was harmed?

The defendants were broken up into three groups to be prosecuted in three different trials, the first of which was scheduled in Judge Kaplan's courtroom in October 2018. Due to his overlapping entanglements, Dawkins was to be a defendant in two of the trials, including the first.

In the courtroom on this morning, the defense was trying to get the charges thrown out before trial, a routine but normally unsuccessful effort at this stage—but in this instance, one that it seemed might have a sliver of a chance. Writing in the legal blog Sidebars, Randall Eliason, a professor at the George Washington School of Law and the former chief of the Fraud and Public Corruption section at the U.S. Attorney's office in the District of Columbia, described the government's case as one that "definitely stretches the limits of criminal fraud."

Michael Schachter, the lawyer for Adidas executive Jim Gatto and a partner in the New York law firm Willkie, Farr & Gallagher, took the lead in making the case for the defendants. "At minimum," he began, "this is an extremely unusual case." He cited precedents that he said should lead to the charges being dismissed—one involving a sports agent named Norby Walters, as well as certain elements of the case against Jeffrey Skilling, the former CEO of Enron. "This theory," he said, referring to the logic of the charges against Gatto and the others, "is even more flawed."

Judge Kaplan, gray-haired, peered down at him from the bench through his wire-rimmed glasses. Over his right shoulder, a little daylight streamed in through a narrow window. He interrupted for the first but not last time. "Then I should just ignore everything in the indictment, right?" he asked. He did not seem to be expecting an answer.

"I'm sorry if I'm exercised here," Schachter apologized when he got a little animated.

"You know, I've actually read the indictments," Kaplan said when Schachter tried to characterize them. The judge paused for a beat. "Carefully," he added.

Schachter pressed on, violating the maxim that when you're in a hole, stop digging. The other defense lawyers could have taken a turn and spoken up, but they seemed to be all but cowering. When Schachter tried to make an additional point, Kaplan stopped him and asked, "Are you kidding me?"

In basketball games, there is a definitive result, a winner and a loser. But this hearing was an incremental step in a long process that would not have an outcome for months or even years—though as one defense lawyer pointed out to me, the defendants had already lost because what was on the tapes was "ruinous to their careers." Who was going to give Book Richardson, Lamont Evans, Tony Bland, or Chuck Person another job in college basketball? Not even their own lawyers were arguing that the assistant coaches had not flagrantly violated the NCAA's recruiting regulations. What was at issue was whether they had committed crimes.

When the cases finally come to trial, juries might be more open to some of the legal arguments than Kaplan was. Prosecutors must make a case according to the existing legal statutes, but to get conviction, they must also tell a story that juries find compelling, and that may be difficult here. In the narrative laid out by government lawyers, there *were* victims—but they were not necessarily the universities. On moral and ethical grounds (if not, perhaps, legal ones), it is the young athletes who look more like victims. Adults were making money off them. In some cases, their own family members were profiting from them. It's not clear how many of the kids received any money, or how much.

Judge Kaplan seemed to indicate that he was eager to put college basketball itself on trial in his courtroom. As Schachter tried to make another point, he stopped him and said, "We all know as a matter of common sense how this industry works. We do, don't we?"

Dawkins was in court that February morning and beautifully put together, as usual—a bespoke khaki-colored suit with a white pocket square over an off-white shirt, though he was a little out of season, as if he were attending a July charity event in the Hamptons.

He is about six feet tall with an athletic-enough-looking build, but he said that suits off the rack do not fit his frame. His light brown shoes came from a boutique in New York. He did not remember exactly where he purchased them, but he did know when— on the day of the NBA draft in 2017, which took place at the Barclays Center in Brooklyn. He somehow made the trip without packing proper footwear.

An aunt of Dawkins's had traveled in from Los Angeles to support him at his court appearance. "His parents are both educators," she said, explaining why they could not be there.

Because he is a part of two of the trials, Dawkins had two hearings to attend. As the lawyers, defendants, and a handful of journalists congregated in the corridors before and after the proceedings, he seemed relaxed and at times even to be enjoying having a small audience. His lawyer, Haney, a longtime family friend from Michigan, was talking during one break about Lou Dawkins's playing career. "Your dad hit the most famous shot in Tulsa history," he said. "He was a damn good player."

"He was serviceable," Dawkins joked in response, adding that over the years the myth of his father's buzzer-beating shot had grown. "It was a normal three-pointer. Now it's like it was from half-court."

Dawkins said that he hoped one day to get back in the basketball business, if not as an agent then perhaps as a consultant of some kind. But he was shut down for now. "No GM is going to talk to me," he said, "but I still talk to my players. They're still cool with me. But when [the FBI] took my phones, I lost a lot of my contacts, so there's some guys I'm just out of touch with."

Like the other defendants and their lawyers, he was whipsawed by Judge Kaplan's unyielding tone, but he did see a bright side in it. "I thought it was going to be boring, and it definitely wasn't boring."

Kaplan had commented from the bench that the assistant coaches among the defendants seemed to have "selfish" motives and were not "acting in the sole interests of the schools." At the same time they were recruiting players, he said, they were acting to advance their own financial well-being and careers. That, in particular, seemed off base to Dawkins. "Isn't that the way the world works?" he said. "Even if you work for somebody you still have to look out for yourself, too, right?"

He said that he had to get permission from the court to travel but had been able to spend some time in Atlanta. Mostly he was living with his parents in Cleveland because that's what his mother wanted. "The way she feels is, when I was out on my own, I got arrested."

Dawkins is affable and funny, and you can see why he was, in his own way, successful. He joked about being under his parents' watch in a city he'd rather not be in. "If I get convicted and have to go to jail," he said, "don't you think I should get some credit for time served for living in Cleveland?"

CHAPTER NINE

WHEN WE SIN AGAINST OUR NATURE

I n the documents filed by prosecutors, individuals not charged with crimes but who figured into the schemes in some way were identified indirectly. Brian Bowen Jr. was "Player-10," but almost immediately after news of the federal investigation broke, media outlets identified him by name. He was, after all, the only player who had committed late in the recruiting season to a "public research university located in Kentucky" with "approximately 22,640 students." (It made you wonder why the prosecutors bothered with the aliases.) Brian Bowen Sr. was called "Father-2," and Pitino, "Coach-2."

Prosecutors quoted media accounts of Bowen's June 3, 2017, announcement that he had chosen Louisville and noted that his decision was considered a "surprise commitment"—that it "came out of nowhere" and was a "late recruiting coup." The government alleged that beginning in May 2017, Dawkins and his associates conspired to funnel $100,000 to Bowen's family in order to influence him to enroll at Louisville. The plan was formulated at the "request and with the assistance of one or more coaches" at Louisville, and the money was to come from Adidas and to be delivered to Brian Bowen Sr., the player's father, in four payments of $25,000 each.

The motivation for such a scheme would go back to the principles established by Sonny Vaccaro, who wanted the programs that his shoe company sponsored to land top players, get on national TV, and advance deep into the NCAA tournament. And it would be in line with the desires of Tom Jurich (even though no one suggests he knew about payoffs), who wanted top players and winning teams to fill the arena and please the deep-pocketed Louisvillians who paid for his luxury boxes and premium seats.

Dawkins and his cohorts knew all that. They understood the industry from top to bottom. They may have been unknown to some of their patrons, but they were fulfilling needs, working behind the scenes, greasing the levers and making everyone happy. They did not always do their work seamlessly—they had serious cash flow problems—or as secretly as they imagined, but they had a handle on all the motivations.

In the transcripts taken from the FBI recordings, Merl Code, like Dawkins, serves as an instructor to those he believes are not as well versed in how college recruiting really works—and as an unwitting narrator for prosecutors. He tells Sood, the Princeton-based Indian American financial advisor and a novice in this game, that he is being introduced to "how stuff happens with kids and getting into particular schools, and so this is kind of one of those instances where we needed to step up and help one of our flagship schools in Louisville, you know, secure a five-star-caliber kid. Obviously, that helps, you know, our potential business."

Code, who worked for Nike before joining Adidas, continues in that same conversation to instruct Sood on the dark art of how to get cash to high school players, stressing that it has to be a chain—with no direct link between the shoe company and the recipient of the money. Adidas, he says, could not be seen as "engaging in a monetary relationship with an amateur athlete. We're engaging in a monetary relationship with a business manager, and whatever he decides to do with it, that's between him and the family." (Munish Sood was one of the ten individuals arrested in the investigation—but one of two who has not been indicted by the Justice Department. He is not a defendant in any of the three scheduled trials and is assumed to be cooperating with prosecutors.)

In their interactions with one another, the defendants give a strong impression of being the types who make promises before they fully think things through and before they tidy up what would seem like crucial details. For example: where the money will come from and how it will be accounted for without raising suspicions. There is a caper element to their day-to-day machinations. On film, the great college basketball scandal of 2017 and 2018 would play as tragicomedy.

Two months after prosecutors say that Brian Bowen Sr. agreed to a deal, and after his son was already on Louisville's campus, he still had not received any of the $100,000 he was promised. It was slow coming from Adidas, so Dawkins and Code persuaded Sood and a person they believed was an associate of Sood's (he was an FBI undercover agent) to front them $25,000, to be reimbursed by Adidas. Code later tells Dawkins the reimbursement seems hung up in the system—and expresses frustration about an email request for "all these PO numbers and vendor numbers and blah blah blah blah blah."

It was the type of bureaucratic nightmare that anyone who works in a corporate setting would recognize. Code's requests for payment kept being spit back to him. He had wanted to route the money through a consulting company he controlled, but the gambit was stymied because Code's firm was not yet in the company's system. Understandably, he hoped to elevate the issue to someone who could just cut through the red tape. He complained to Dawkins that he wished Gatto would just "flex his muscle and push it through the system, but that's obviously not what's happening."

Any reporter who has ever covered a mob trial or a criminal case made with secret recordings knows that there are always moments of dark comedy captured on the tapes—some poor schlub, caught on a wiretap or hidden microphone, who says something along the lines of, "I really hope we're not being recorded." In the light of day, such statements are not generally helpful to criminal defendants. On the wiretaps, the defendants in the basketball case do indeed give some worry to covering their tracks. Code says he might have to "lean on" an unidentified Adidas executive, someone senior to Gatto, and get him to execute "some of his side hustle off-the-books shit" to finance the reimbursement. He makes it clear that for reasons of "cleanliness and lack of questions," the money transfer to Bowen Sr. had to be in cash. Dawkins says, "Obviously, we have to put funding out, and obviously some of it can't be completely accounted for on paper because some of it is, whatever you want to call it, illegal." On July 11, the FBI undercover agent, Sood's supposed partner, showed up at Sood's Princeton office with $25,000 in cash. They seemed to have grown impatient waiting for

Adidas to come up with the money. Two days later, Sood passed on $19,500 of it to Brian Bowen Sr. at a restaurant near Newark International Airport in what the government termed a "handoff." It was the first of what was supposed to be four installments.

Dawkins also seems to have promised additional money— again, without knowing what its source would be. He told an undercover agent in a phone conversation that although the deal for Brian Bowen Jr. was done, "basically, we just need to take care of his dad with two grand monthly. . . . I just gotta figure out how to get the two grand to him every month."

The last week of July 2017 was the apex of the summer grassroots basketball season—and a moment when the government collected some of its most damaging information regarding Louisville. Three massive tournaments—the Adidas Fab 48, the Super 64, and the Bigfoot Las Vegas Classic—were all in progress at the same time. Hundreds of teams and thousands of players descended on the desert from just about every state in the nation, as well as from Europe, South America, New Zealand, Australia, and Africa. The temperature hit 107 degrees that week, but the games, like everything else in Las Vegas in the summer, took place in well-chilled indoor spaces. The players ranged in age from high schoolers all the way down to third graders, and the games attracted head coaches and their assistants from just about every Division I basketball program in the NCAA.

Christian Dawkins set up shop in a hotel on the Strip. On July 27, prosecutors say, he met with Marty Blazer; Jonathan Brad Augustine, who was the director of an AAU program in Florida that produced a steady stream of college players; and the undercover agent posing as Blazer's associate. The government notes, "Prior to the meeting, the FBI placed video recorders inside of the hotel room."

The fifth person in the meeting was Jordan Fair, then twenty-six years old, an assistant coach at Louisville who was previously the head coach at Oldsmar Christian School in Florida, his alma mater, before Pitino hired him in 2016. Fair attended three different colleges, graduating from St. Petersburg College in Florida. At the University of North Florida, where he played basketball his freshman year, his bio in the media guide said that the "person he would most like to meet" was Michael Jordan and his ambition was to play basketball overseas and eventually become a college coach.

Oldsmar Christian, near Tampa, was a mecca for top players and a good place for a coach hoping to advance in his profession. In just four years, Fair won 115 games against just 32 losses, and seventeen of his kids earned Division I scholarships. It was unusual for Pitino to pluck someone right from high school coaching and put him on his staff, but as he explained after hiring Fair, "I first came across Jordan while recruiting some of his players. I was extremely impressed with his practices, his organizational skills, and the way he related to his players."

Fair had intended to make an impression. He said that whenever college coaches came into his gym, he regarded it as an audition. Pitino gave him a job as a "program assistant" and the next season promoted him to become one of his three assistant coaches. "I take every practice and every workout in front of college coaches as a job interview," he told the *Louisville-Courier Journal* after first joining Pitino's staff. "He just brought up a couple of positions that he had and asked if I'd be interested. God has blessed me; there's no better place to get into this thing than with someone like Coach Pitino."

Not long after Fair got his promotion, replacing a Pitino assistant, Mike Balado, who left to become head coach at Arkansas State, Pitino said that Fair was already proving himself as a formidable recruiter. "We've had assistants move on and sometimes you're happy for them, but that hurts continuity," he said. "And that's where the so-called operations guys or graduation assistants come in, a guy like Jordan Fair, for instance. Mike Balado leaves, and he had a lot to do with our future recruiting, but Jordan Fair comes in and he's a big-time recruiter and he fills that void right away."

Prosecutors described what occurred during the July 27 meeting in Vegas. With Fair in the room, Dawkins began talking about a player in the high school class of 2019—the class after Brian Bowen Jr.—whom he was trying to direct to Louisville. According to the criminal complaint, Dawkins "laid out the plan to funnel money to the family of the player, and said, 'The mom is like . . . we need our fucking money. So we got to be able to fund the situation. . . . We're all working together to get the kid to Louisville. Obviously, in turn, the kid will come back to us.'"

Dawkins noted that because Louisville was already on NCAA probation, they had to be careful. At this point, the complaint says, Fair agreed, adding, "We gotta be very low key." Dawkins then said that the plan "works on every angle. We have Merl at Adidas, we have Brad out with the kid, and we have Louisville." The reference to Louisville, the document says, was made as Dawkins nodded in the direction of Fair.

Augustine suggested that the easiest way to get payments to this player would be to direct the money through his AAU program. The undercover agent handed Augustine an envelope with $12,700 in cash, the complaint says. After that, Augustine said that he expected Adidas to contribute a significant amount for the player because they would want to help Pitino and Louisville. "No one swings a bigger dick than Pitino" at Adidas, Augustine said, according to the criminal complaint. He added that all Pitino had to do was "pick up the phone and call somebody [and say] these are my guys, [and] they're taking care of us."

After Jordan Fair left the room, the discussion turned back to the subject of Brian Bowen Jr. Dawkins recalled that the money they had first agreed to pay his family had needed to be increased, because after they settled on a number, a rival athletic company "was coming in with a higher number." According to Dawkins, he reached out to Pitino directly at that point and informed him, "I need you to call Jim Gatto," in order to secure more money and make sure that the deal to get Bowen to Louisville would be consummated.

On May 27, according to the FBI, Gatto had two phone conversations "with a phone number used by Pitino." On June 1, he had a third conversation with someone at the same number. Two days later, Brian Bowen Jr. announced he was going to Louisville.

Augustine was among the ten people arrested—and is one of the two, along with Sood, who has not been indicted and is not a defendant in any of the trials. It appears that he never passed on the cash that was intended as payments to players or their families, and therefore could not be prosecuted for bribery.

In a court hearing, Gatto's lawyer, Michael Schachter, pointed out that avarice seemed to have prevented at least one of the bribery schemes from reaching completion. "Mr. Augustine had no intention of taking any money and handing it to" the father of a Florida high school player, its purported purpose. "Effectively, he was in his own scheme to rip off Mr. Gatto."

In the narrative laid out by the government, it is possible at various times to conclude that some of the defendants seemed to be trying to pocket money that had another intended purpose—a not uncommon occurrence among people who are charged with illicit activity. Defendants, however, are rarely acquitted just because they are not honest with one another.

After the arrests were made, the charges filed, and the news blasted that the FBI and the Justice Department had moved against college basketball, Brian Bowen Jr. was summoned to New York to be interviewed by federal law enforcement agents. He was a month into the fall semester at Louisville and had been participating in workouts and playing in pickup games with his future teammates in advance of the start of full-squad practices, which were less than a week away.

He was having fun, easing his way into campus life and already feeling comfortable. His parents were nearby. Just as they had moved nearly two decades ago from Saginaw to East Lansing to follow his cousin Jason Richardson, the future NBA player—and later to Indiana to be near Bowen's prep school—now they moved to Louisville and into a downtown high-rise called the Galt House. It was both a residence and a hotel—in fact, the official hotel of Churchill Downs and the Kentucky Derby.

Among coaches and other college basketball insiders, it is viewed as a red flag when players' parents relocate to the college town, especially when they do not take jobs there. The obvious question is:

How are they supporting themselves? It's not at all uncommon, but it advertises possible irregularities.

Tugs's family found him a lawyer—Jason Setchen, of Miami, who specializes in representing athletes in disputes with the NCAA. He had represented current NFL quarterback Cam Newton when his eligibility was under threat at Auburn because of money his father had allegedly accepted from an agent. This, however, was different and more serious. Brian Bowen Jr. was being interviewed as a witness in a criminal investigation. On the way to New York, Setchen told him: We're taking a trip. Let's make this as fun as we can. They walked all over the city. They went to sneaker stores. To Chinatown. To Ground Zero and the 9/11 Tribute Museum.

The next day, Tugs was sitting in a conference room full of FBI agents and prosecutors. What did he know? Did he personally take any money? Why had he delayed his choice so long? What did he know about conversations between his father and Pitino? Between his dad and other Louisville coaches? How about other kids in his recruiting class? Did he have information on how they made their choices and why? Had he ever heard of Jim Gatto or Merl Code?

Every person in the room was white. There was a picture in the room of some old-timey New York scene, of aristocratic types in top hats. They were all white. It was all unfamiliar, disorienting, and terrifying.

Tugs told the federal agents that he had not received any money. He had not been part of any conversations about bribes to influence his decision. Whatever his father had or had not done, he didn't know anything about it.

He flew back to Louisville. His teammates started practice without their head coach, Pitino, who had been suspended and then terminated; without Jordan Fair and another assistant coach,

Kenny Johnson, both of whom were ultimately also fired; and without him. With Tom Jurich also fired, Louisville's new interim athletic director told Bowen he could not practice or compete with the team, pending further investigation.

He was allowed to use the weight room in the basketball center, but not under the supervision of the team's training staff. He felt like an intramural player. He worked out five days a week at a gym in a Baptist church a few miles off campus with a private trainer, Derek Anderson, a former player at Kentucky, because he needed someone to "kick him in the butt," as Setchen said. But the workouts were lonely and, over time, they felt pointless.

He had wanted to gain weight and muscle, but if anything, he was going in the wrong direction. His shot was going flat. "I'm doing drills to keep my handle tight," he said at the time, meaning his ball handling, but that was hard when he was on the court alone instead of dribbling in traffic against defenders.

In early November, Setchen met with Louisville's NCAA compliance staff and other administrators to try to persuade them to let Bowen play. The FBI, he said, had cleared Tugs. With all that material gathered in wiretapped phone calls and secretly recorded hotel-room meetings, and all the discussion over money and where to make the handoffs, his voice was not on any of the recordings and he wasn't in any of the rooms. Setchen argued that it was his father's deal, not his.

Walter Byers became the NCAA's first executive director in 1951 and stayed in the job until 1987, and for most of that time he was the apostle of amateurism in college sport—a powerful and persuasive voice for keeping the competition pure, as he defined it. Under his leadership, and to the current day, the organization has had a zero tolerance policy with regard to athletes or their families taking even small sums of money, and its measures in response to perceived violations are punitive and often breathtakingly heartless.

In 2011, the NCAA's enforcement division discovered that the mother of a Baylor basketball player, Perry Jones, had accepted a fifteen-day, $1,195 loan from his AAU coach to avoid being evicted from her apartment—a loan which at that point she had already paid back. She was battling a heart condition and was unable to work, and the family at times had stayed in hotel rooms they paid for by the week. Her son did not know about the loan, but the NCAA ruled him ineligible for his postseason conference tournament and for the first five games of the next season. "Basically, I got suspended because we were struggling, and my mom didn't want us to live on the streets," Jones said. "We were down to nothing and someone helped us out."

As he neared the end of his tenure, Byers began to express doubts, and by the end of his life he was a harsh critic of the organization he built. In 1984, he said he believed that up to 30 percent of the major universities were cheating (an estimate many would say was way too low), and he proposed creating an "open division" of semiprofessional programs. Later that year, he told *Sports Illustrated*, "I'm gradually coming to the conclusion that there has to be a major rearrangement on the part of the institutions of higher learning as to what they want to do with their athletic programs. I think there's an inherent conflict that has to be resolved. I'm not prepared to go into how an open division would work. But we're in a situation where we, the colleges, say it's improper for athletes to get, for example, a new car. Well, is that morally wrong? Or is it wrong because we say it's wrong?"

Byers, a native of Kansas City who was an assistant sports information director for the Big Ten Conference before taking the top
job at the NCAA, well understood the power of words. The most
shocking aspect of his late-in-life conversion was his disavowal of
the term "student-athlete," which he had coined, and which remains the organization's mantra—its rationale for existing and
what allegedly distinguishes college from professional sports.

In his 1995 memoir, *Unsportsmanlike Conduct: Exploiting College Athletes,* Byers wrote, "We crafted the term *student-athlete,*
and soon it was embedded in all NCAA rules and interpretations as
a mandated substitute for such words as players and athletes. We
told college publicists to speak of 'college teams' and not football or
basketball 'clubs,' a term common to the pros."

Byers admitted that "student-athlete" did double duty: It was
the phrase that evoked the NCAA's myth of amateurism, and it also
helped to shield the organization from having to pay for athletes
injured during competition. In the mid-1950s, a football player
named Ray Dennison died from head injuries suffered while playing in a game for Fort Lewis A&M in Colorado. His widow applied
for workmen's compensation benefits but was denied them by Colorado's Supreme Court, which ruled that he was not an employee
"since the college was not in the football business" and had not
fielded a team "for the purpose of making a profit."

Even though the ruling was in favor of the college, NCAA lawyers continued to be spooked by the implications of its players
being categorized as employees, and they considered the term
"student-athlete" to be legally protective. And it has been, in numerous cases in which the NCAA and its members prevailed in legal battles against severely injured athletes. In one, a running back
for Texas Christian University, Kent Waldrep, was paralyzed from

the neck down in a 1974 game against Alabama after being hit by multiple tacklers, then fought a marathon legal battle against TCU for benefits. It ended in 2000, when an appeals court ruled that he was not an employee because he had not paid taxes on his scholarship.

Referring to the Ray Dennison case, Walter Byers wrote, "I wonder what that same court's decision would have been if [Dennison], receiving a Big Eight Conference full ride, had died in the 1990 Orange Bowl, as Colorado lost to Notre Dame in a game sponsored by Federal Express for a rights payment of $2,035,411, televised by NBC for $6,150,000, watched by 74,705 spectators who paid $2,140,870 for tickets. The gross take split among the not-for-profit colleges and Orange Bowl committee was $10,765,859."

In bringing the current NCAA basketball case, Joon Kim, then the interim U.S. attorney in New York, said the defendants had "sullied the spirit of amateur athletics." In court documents, prosecutors quoted the NCAA rulebook extensively, and in doing so, they called attention to stated principles that sound antiquated if not outright absurd. "Among the NCAA's core principles for the conduct of intercollegiate athletics is a directive that 'student athletes shall be amateurs in an intercollegiate sport,'" the criminal complaint says, and that "'student athletes should be protected from exploitation by professional and commercial enterprises.'"

The words read almost like a joke, considering that the NCAA itself is a commercial and exploitive enterprise. The indictment notes that the NCAA and its member institutions are in the business of making money: "The scheme . . . interfered with the universities' ability to control their assets and created a risk of tangible economic harm" as it related to, among other matters, "the possible disgorgement of certain profit sharing."

In the fiscal year ending in 2017, the NCAA for the first time surpassed $1 billion in revenue. The majority of its income, $761 million, came from television rights for the season-ending basketball tournament, an annual payment that increased to $869 million in 2018. The contract with CBS and its partners stretches to 2032 and has an overall value of almost $19.6 billion.

That money, though, is just a fraction of what is generated by college athletes in the sports of football and men's basketball. Their labor is responsible for revenue that flows directly to their universities (not to the NCAA) from a range of sources, including ticket sales, donations from wealthy boosters, in-stadium advertising, conference broadcast rights, and money from the shoe companies.

The newest moneymaking gambit is conference-specific TV networks that broadcast games, highlight shows, coaches' shows, and sports talk, feeding the unquenchable appetites of college sports fans for content. They will generate additional billions of dollars in revenue.

The schools cannot directly market the images of the players, but they find ways around it. Before superstar prospect Ben Simmons played his one season at LSU, the university paid for billboards around Baton Rouge that said "25 Is Coming," a reference to his uniform number. (Simmons later said he regretted that the NBA's age limit prevented him from going straight from high school into the pros. At LSU, he said, "I'd have class, go lift, go to practice, and 'Oh, Ben, you've got to stay and do media and the photo shoot.' So I'd be kind of annoyed, like, 'What am I getting out of this?'")

Universities reap tens of millions of dollars in student fees—taxes charged on their students solely for the privilege of attending institutions with big-time sports programs, regardless of whether they care about the games or can secure a ticket to attend them. In addition, the effort and sweat of college athletes throws off money in many other directions—to the NCAA's broadcast partners, to gambling interests, to hotels and restaurants that fill up when they play. CBS, TNT, and other outlets that televise the NCAA tournament gross more than $1 billion in advertising over the course of the three-week event. In March 2017, $422 million was bet on basketball at Las Vegas's legal sports books—with the bookmakers reaping $21.5 million in profits—compared to $138.4 million bet on the Super Bowl. In total, an estimated $10 billion is wagered on the tournament, some of it legally in the United States, but the vast majority going to offshore sports bookies and local bookmakers, according to the American Gaming Association.

College football generates even more revenue than basketball, but the money does not flow through the NCAA because the top football programs essentially seceded from their longtime governing organization in 1998 when they came together to form the Bowl Championship Series. The schools in the BCS are now referred to as the Power Five conferences, and include traditional Southeastern Conference powers like Alabama, Georgia, Florida, and Auburn; Big Ten behemoths Ohio State and Michigan; Stanford and Oregon in the Pac-12; and one independent, Notre Dame. But the players still compete under the NCAA's student-athlete rubric, and their compensation is limited to the value of their scholarships and modest "cost of attendance" stipends intended to allow them to afford a trip or two back home, the occasional off-campus meal, and day-to-day incidentals. (The intent is for athletes from impoverished backgrounds to be able to live a little more like their wealthier classmates.)

The current ten-year contract between the Power Five conferences and ESPN to televise bowl games is worth $7.2 billion but could go up significantly if the BCS expands to an eight-team rather than four-team postseason playoff. There is, as well, enormous money in college football's regular season. The athletic departments at both Texas and Ohio State now surpass $60 million in ticket sales, most of it from football. At least ten university athletic departments exceed $125 million in total revenue, with Texas A&M first on the list, at $192 million.

The Power Five schools are generally assumed to have a built-in advantage in basketball because of their enormous football revenue. However, relatively small Catholic institutions continue to compete at the top level, including Villanova, the national champion in basketball two of the last three years, and Xavier, a No. 1 seed in the 2018 NCAA tournament. Gonzaga, a Jesuit university in Spokane, Washington, is another perennial basketball power. It is an oddity on the college sports landscape, but also a hint of something larger: The money is not always about the pursuit of victory. The money, to an equal extent, is just about the money—and the ability of the people who raise it to skim off huge chunks of it to pay themselves big salaries.

In 2013, the National College Players Association, a fledgling union of NCAA athletes, published a study in cooperation with sports economists at Drexel University in Philadelphia, titled "The $6 Billion Heist: Robbing College Athletes Under the Guise of Amateurism." Using the percentage of team revenues allocated to players' salaries in the NFL and NBA, they calculated what NCAA athletes at the major programs would earn if they got the same share of revenue as the pros did.

For the ten top-revenue teams in college football, their lost wages over a four-year period ranged from $1.6 million for a player at Arkansas to $2.2 million at Texas. In basketball, with far fewer players per team, the "heist" was much greater. The range was $2.7 million per player in uncompensated labor at Indiana up to $6.5 million at the top school—Louisville.

As nonprofit entities, college athletic departments have an incentive not to reflect any substantial profit. The most obvious way they spend down their largesse is on the lavish salaries they award to coaches. The $11 million that Alabama football coach Nick Saban made in 2017, which included a $4 million "signing bonus" attached to his new, eight-year deal, was more than any coach in the NFL earned in 2017, including Bill Belichick of the New England Patriots, who has led his team to five Super Bowl titles. Belichick made $7.5 million—almost $4 million less than Saban.

You could argue that Alabama pays Saban his market value, but is there another university that would pay him that? Or an NFL team that would pay him $3 million more than its current highest-paid coach? (His record in two years as coach of the NFL's Miami Dolphins was 15–17.) The better explanation is that his salary is a way to unload some of the cash his program brings to the institution. In 2017, Alabama football accounted for $108.2 million in revenue—and a staggering $45.9 million in profit.

NCAA Division I programs also pay bundles of money for coaches *not* to coach—in buyouts after they have been fired before the end of their contracts. In 2017, the Power Five football programs were committed to a total of $69 million to dismissed coaches, according to figures compiled by Fox Sports analyst Joel Klatt. He calculated that if they spread that money around to their players, each would receive $10,000.

The bloated buyouts even flow in the wake of disgrace. Baylor University paid its former football coach, Art Briles, $15.1 million after he was fired in 2016 following the revelations that numerous players were involved in sexual assaults, including an alleged gang rape. When Ken Starr, the former university president, left Baylor, he came away with a $4.5 million payout.

More often, NCAA coaches are bought out for perceived under-performance and in the hope of bringing in a new man who can recruit higher-quality players and win more games. After the 2018 season, Memphis fired basketball coach Tubby Smith, whose career record includes 597 wins and a national title. In two years at Memphis he went 40–26, but his squads did not qualify for the NCAA tournament. The cost of buying out the remainder of his contract came to about $10 million.

His replacement, Penny Hardaway, was a beloved former Memphis player and a four-time NBA all-star with one other significant attraction: He was the head coach of both a high school and a grass-roots team in Memphis, and one of his players, six-foot-eleven forward James Wiseman, was ESPN's top-ranked prospect in the class of 2019. There was no guarantee Hardaway could sign Wiseman, or any of the other top young prospects he coached, but he seemed like the best chance to make basketball relevant again and put fans back in the Pyramid, the 20,000-seat arena where Memphis games had been drawing puny crowds of 6,000 or less of late.

In each of Pitino's last three years, the basketball program turned a profit of about $30 million, far and away the highest of any college team. They played in an NBA-sized arena with NBA-like amenities. By contrast, the NBA's thirty teams averaged only about $17 million in net income in 2017, and nine of them are said to have lost money. (If they did not pay their players, of course, every NBA team would be profitable, wildly so.) A handful of NBA coaches earn more than the $7.8 million that Pitino was making, including the highest paid, San Antonio's Gregg Popovich, at $11 million. But the vast majority make substantially less and are in the $2 million to $5 million range.

In a 2016 article, ESPN investigative journalist Paula Lavigne wrote about the other uses that universities find for sports revenue: "Powered by multimillion-dollar media rights contracts and rising ticket-sales revenue, the richest schools have spent aggressively: on private jets, on campus perks like barber shops and bowling alleys, on biometric gadgets for athletes, and on five-star hotel stays during travel. They've also hired a plethora of athletic department support staffers who earn six-figure salaries and sometimes have obscure job titles such as 'horticulturalist' and 'museum curator.'"

Columnist Tim Sullivan of the *Louisville Courier-Journal* has been a close observer of the University of Louisville's athletic department. "They don't want to make a profit," he said. "The goal is to have fabulous facilities, elite coaches, championship teams, and lose a dime."

College basketball's underworld, consisting of agents, runners, shoe companies, and shady coaches, is not a corrective to the contradictions of the NCAA's gospel of amateurism. It is exploitation piled on top of exploitation.

First of all, the money—even if it reaches the athletes—is a pittance compared to what is generated by the games. Based on Louisville's $45.6 million in basketball revenue in 2017, and the NBA's union-bargained formula of paying the players roughly half the team's take, each of its thirteen scholarship players was worth an average of about $1.7 million a year. As a five-star recruit and likely starter, you could argue that Bowen should have been paid more.

The court documents indicate that of the $100,000 promised to Brian Bowen Sr., just $19,500 seems to have been delivered at the time the FBI made its arrests and the scheme came to a halt. Considering the struggles that Dawkins and company experienced in raising money for the payoffs, it's not clear if they ever would have been able to fully fund the $100,000 promise.

That the defendants seem to have been buying players on the cheap, however, is not the most odious aspect of the criminal case. There are indications that Dawkins and others were using young athletes as bargaining chips, by attempting to direct current high school prospects to particular college teams in return for access to their current players. The goal was to have an inside track on managing the business affairs of players who were soon to jump to the NBA.

As he traveled the country, Dawkins was in the habit of emailing back to his employer, Andy Miller, and to others at the ASM sports agency. The emails were obtained from the prosecution by defense lawyers as part of the discovery process. Some of them were viewed as well by Pete Thamel and Pat Forde of Yahoo News, whose reporting since September 2017 has led much of the daily coverage of the unfolding scandal. Their story on the emails refers to them as "a diary of the basketball black market."

In one August 2016 email, with the subject line "morning update," Dawkins wrote to agent Andrew Vye that Lauri Markkanen, a talented seven-foot forward from Finland who was soon to start his freshman season at Arizona, had not yet settled on an agent. (Since he was a college player, NCAA rules would technically have prohibited him from signing or accepting benefits from an agent.)

He suggested that Vye reach out to the Arizona coaching staff and dangle Brian Bowen Jr., then about to enter his senior year of high school, as bait. If he sent Bowen to them, he hoped that they would persuade Markkanen to sign with Miller's agency. "The kid that they want from me is Brian Bowen," he said, adding, "Arizona will do pretty much whatever we ask of them right now, until my kid decides on a school."

He emailed Andy Miller that he was also in contact with assistant coaches at two other schools to see if he could get some of their players for the agency in return for Bowen. "Trying to close the deal on Brian Bowen for Michigan State," he said. "Trying to do a trade deal for Gary Harris, Miles Bridges, etc." And in a separate email to Miller: "Trying to close the deal on Brian Bowen for Indiana. I told him if we can work together and if he can push for us to get Thomas Bryant and OG Anunoby two projected first rounders from IU this year we can work something out."

The emails may help explain why Bowen waited until the last possible moment before he committed. To the extent that Dawkins was running his recruitment, the longer it went on, the more he could use him as bait to get access to college coaches and their current rosters.

Other emails that Dawkins sent touted his connections to various coaches, current NCAA players, high school kids, and their families. Several of the emails were expense requests—for reimbursements for a $400 ATM withdrawal labeled as an "advance" for the mother of a top high schooler, and for meals or hotel rooms for players and their families. After attending a Nike Skills camp, Dawkins sent back expenses as well as performance reviews for four players whom he labeled "our guys."

There is probably a zero chance that Dawkins was telling the truth about every scheme he had in progress and every coach and family he had in his pocket. It is in his personality to promise the world and figure it out later—to use one relationship to make another. It's the nature of his line of work. He may have invented some of his associations and embellished others. In some of the emails, he may just have been sending along accounts of supposed business meals in order to cheat on his expenses.

When the cases get to trial, jurors will have to sort it out. Is Dawkins a reliable narrator? They will determine the consequences for those who have been charged. None of them are head coaches—even though the names of several at high-profile programs are mentioned in the secretly recorded conversations. Some of the defense attorneys have wondered how they evaded prosecution. "This is like Enron, except if they only charged the secretaries," Dawkins's attorney, Steve Haney, said.

T om Konchalski would attend a second court appearance for Jim Gatto and expected to sit through every day of his trial. "I want to be of support," he said. He had known Gatto a long time, and the sixty-five-year-old Pitino even longer, from when Pitino was in his early twenties and just starting to make his bones in the coaching profession.

Konchalski believed that both of them were caught up in a climate of moral rot. But he did not absolve Pitino, who for many years, he said, embodied the spirit of a proper basketball man. No one was better on the practice court. No one cared more about seeing the game played correctly, down to the smallest details. The assistant coaches he hired approached the game the same way, and if a kid, for example, set a screen incorrectly—not at the proper angle—they were on him just as fast as he was. And everybody stayed in the gym until the screen was set correctly. And until every other player on the court understood the way they were supposed to do it.

Herb Sendek, now the coach at Santa Clara, his fourth head coaching job, remembers working for Pitino as a graduate assistant at Providence, an apprenticeship role, and early on attending a staff meeting in which Pitino was seeking input on how they should defend the four corners offense, the stalling tactic employed before the shot clock came to college basketball. "He got upset with me because I didn't have any good answers," Sendek said. "Even though it was my first year and we hadn't even started practice yet, he expected me to contribute, significantly. In all honesty, I was not prepared to, but he held me to the highest standard and expected me to do things. I thought, 'This guy is unreasonable. How can he expect me to do that?' But it made me grow faster."

As his assistants mature and are ready for the next step, Sendek said, "He goes to the wall to get you a job."

Pitino is proud of the young coaches he hired and trained, and his "coaching tree"—the assistants who have gone on to top jobs in the NCAA and NBA—is as impressive as any in basketball. Mike Balado came on to Pitino's staff in 2013. It was his eighth job as a college assistant coach, along a career path that began at junior colleges and Division II schools, but hooking on with Pitino elevated him to a different level. When he was hired as head coach at Arkansas State in 2017, the school's athletic director talked about how fortunate the program was to attract someone from Pitino's staff, calling it "a great tribute to our emerging brand."

Over the course of Pitino's long career, the profession has moved in a new direction. One common expression now is that the outcomes of NCAA tournament games are determined by "who wins in July"—meaning which coaches get the best take of players from the big summer tournaments in Las Vegas and elsewhere.

Head coaches hire assistants who are recruiters first, some of whom came straight out of the grassroots scene, where the quality of basketball is notoriously bad. The coaches tend not to be teachers of the game. They are at home in Christian Dawkins's world, and their job is to sign players.

"Pitino's credo was no shortcuts," Konchalski said. "But then he started bringing in coaches without the same qualifications of those he used to hire. They were recruiters first and coaches second. Maybe he felt it's something he had to do to stay competitive. I can't say. But we all get in trouble when we sin against our nature."

CHAPTER TEN

"I FEEL IT WAS AN ASSASSINATION"

Even as prosecutors were still laying out the charges that morning in New York, calls went out among Pitino's friends. One would say to another: Are you watching? No? Then you better turn your TV on.

Those who tuned in knew instantly what they were witnessing: the end of the Pitino era. Considering what he had already survived—two sex scandals, one involving him directly and the other his team—they recognized it as his third strike. Pitino did not. His outsized competitive drive always made him believe he could "win" at anything, prevail even when others saw that the game was over.

Pitino was summoned to the office of Greg Postel, the university's interim president. The meeting lasted no more than five minutes. He went back to his office to find that the locks on the door had been changed, as had the locks at the offices of two of his assistant coaches, Jordan Fair and Kenny Johnson. He could not retrieve his personal belongings. He called his wife, Joanne, and told her to quickly gather a few things and meet him at the airport. They almost immediately put their house on the market and it sold in two weeks.

Their charter flight landed in Florida and they took a car to their home on Indian Creek Island, off the coast of Miami. Pitino liked the finer things, and this house, purchased when he was with the Celtics, was his greatest indulgence. A speck of land in Biscayne Bay, the private island has thirty-five residences, all with waterfront views, arranged around a golf and country club. Pitino's 12,000-square-foot Mediterranean-style house, on a 1.25-acre lot, had ten bedrooms, ten bathrooms, a gym, a four-car garage, and a motor court. His neighbors included not just Julio Iglesias and Carl Icahn, but also the billionaire car dealer and art collector Norman Braman, who once owned the Philadelphia Eagles. Beyoncé and Jay-Z were former neighbors. *Forbes* magazine referred to the community as a "billionaire's bunker" protected by a private police force that patrols "via boat, jeep and jet ski 24 hours a day."

From the outside looking in, the island enclave may seem like an ideal place to decamp after a professional and personal blow, but Pitino was agitated and angry. He had lived according to the demands of his job and the rhythms of the basketball seasons, and now all of that was disrupted without warning. "His head was a calendar," his friend Terry Meiners, the Louisville radio host, said. "He'd say, 'I'll meet you at a certain bar on 65th and Lexington,' and give you a date and time, and he wouldn't write it down, but you'd show up six weeks later and he was sitting right there. For forty years every one of his days was spoken for, but now he's a balloon in the wind. He's unemployed and unemployable in college basketball."

People worried about him. They called and texted. About a month after he was fired, Pitino took a trip to Southern California to hang out at Del Mar racetrack and watch the Breeders Cup, and a handful of friends joined him. The trip, Meiners said, "filled his dance card for a few days, but after that, he was back in the same place. I don't think he had any idea what to do with himself."

I talked on the phone to Pitino in mid-January. He was at his house on Indian Creek Island. I asked how he was spending his days. "I think that anytime you get assassinated you like to rest in peace," he replied. "That's the way I look at it. I'm resting in peace. I feel it was an assassination by lots of different venues. I'm not a bitter or a revengeful person. I've never been fired before. I have some ill feelings toward certain people and I think a lot of people would understand why. That's life. I don't have self-pity. A lot of people have it a lot worse."

He said he was doing a lot of reading. He was playing golf and going out on his boat. "I'm quite busy," he said. "I'm also in the midst of selling a house and buying a house." He was buying in Fort Lauderdale and giving up the Indian Creek Island estate. It felt too big. As one of the island's more modest properties, it was on the market for $24 million.

He said he did not understand the FBI's interest in college basketball when it seemed to him they had more important things to investigate, and besides, he believed that what they discovered was what a lot of people already knew. "In every industry, the legal industry, Wall Street, any business, there is always a small percentage of people that doesn't do things the right way. This has been going on in college. The NCAA is having its committee," he said derisively, referring to a blue-ribbon "Commission on College Basketball" appointed by NCAA president Mark Emmert in the wake of the federal charges. Its members included former secretary of state Condoleezza Rice and former NCAA and NBA greats David Robinson and Grant Hill.

In Pitino's view, everything in the federal case has been in clear view for a long time. "Why now? I told them the AAU was too involved. You have to have a camp," he said, meaning the NCAA should sponsor its own events for high school prospects rather than leaving it to the sneaker companies. "They knew the problems."

Pitino has spent most of his life connected to the NCAA, and his association with it and college basketball has made him a rich man. But he now routinely refers to the organization as "a joke." He does not respect the penalties the NCAA imposed for past infractions relating to his team. The current federal case, he believes, involves behaviors that have been going on for decades—though not in his programs.

The problems in his program at Louisville, he said, occurred because people he hired did exactly what he had told them not to do. He had specified red lines that could not be crossed, and they either did not hear him or just ignored his warnings—to catastrophic effect. The basketball program was devastated, the athletic department thrown into chaos, the university humiliated. In the business world, to have subordinates who cause such enormous damage is a marker of poor leadership, and executives get fired for it. Pitino does not see it that way. He believes he had hired well over the course of his career, brilliantly, but was done in by just a couple of mistakes.

"You have to understand. I have had over thirty assistant coaches become head coaches, pro and college." He ticked off several of his accomplished former assistants: Frank Vogel, coach of the NBA's Orlando Magic. "He was my student manager and then an assistant." Brett Brown, the Philadelphia 76ers head coach, who played for him way back at Boston University. Billy Donovan, his former player point guard at Providence, winner of two NCAA titles as coach at Florida and now head man for the NBA's Oklahoma City Thunder. Ralph Willard, who had been his assistant with the New York Knicks and at two college stops and had coached three NCAA teams of his own. "There's twenty-seven others. I have to take full accountability for hiring two guys who were taught to do it the right way and they did it the wrong way. I take full responsibility in that regard."

In the letter notifying Pitino that he was fired, one of the stated reasons was that he had welcomed Christian Dawkins to campus without notifying the university that a sports agent was on the premises. Because Dawkins was "someone known to have acted as an 'agent' for athletes, the basketball staff should have notified Athletics Compliance," the letter states. "No notification was provided."

Dawkins was a widely known figure on the recruiting circuit, from his teenage years as a tournament promoter and recruiting guru, to his role drumming up business for International Management Advisors, the Cleveland firm headed by LeBron James's former financial advisor, and later as the enterprising and energetic runner for high-profile NBA agent Andy Miller. But Pitino said he was not among those who were familiar with Dawkins's business activities. He only remembered him from having been involved with the recruitment of one of his former players. "I didn't know him," he said. "He texted me like five years back about this kid

Jaylen Johnson." Pitino said he knew Andy Miller, but "I never knew [Dawkins] worked for Andy Miller."

As Pitino described it, he and the Bowens had both made their own separate calculation that led Brian Bowen Jr. on a path to Louisville. Bowen wanted playing time, and Arizona, one of the schools on his list, had several players who decided to return rather than go to the NBA. Pitino had lost a key player to the NBA and had a spot to fill. "With Arizona, [Allonzo] Trier and the other kids were staying," Pitino said. "I thought, well, I've seen him once, and Donovan Mitchell"—a Louisville player from the previous season—"is going pro, so we'll bring him in and talk. He was a choirboy. The kid was quiet and respectful."

It is surprising that Pitino—the streetwise New Yorker, immersed in basketball recruiting for four decades, already deeply skeptical about the irregularities that occur right under the nose of the NCAA—would not have gotten a certain feeling from Dawkins when they were in the same room together. That he would not have known the business Dawkins was in, or at least suspected it. But he insists he did not. He took Dawkins's presence at face value—that he was a family friend who had just come along to help.

He did not understand the FBI's interest in college basketball, considering the other pressing matters on its docket. "What is that?" he said. "We're paying for this? I'm a New Yorker. I lost my best friend and brother-in-law in 9/11. What is the FBI doing messing around college basketball and indicting assistant coaches?" (Self-serving as his thoughts may be, others in both the media and the legal community have raised the same question.)

Pitino said that he had passed a polygraph test arranged by his legal team. "I immediately took a lie detector test. By an ex-FBI agent. He asked me two questions. 'Did you have any knowledge of any payments by Adidas to the Bowen family? Did you have any knowledge of illegal activities or money funneling to players?' I passed that."

He did not understand why the unusual trajectory of Bowen's recruitment should reflect on his own methods or integrity. "Here's the story with Bowen. I said at the press conference, I had a player fall in my lap. What idiotic coach would do that and say that if a guy was getting paid money?"

At that press conference in the spring of 2017, he said, "It's funny how it works out. Sometimes there's no explanation. The family said, 'We know what you're all about.' That's really refreshing for us to hear. We've been through a lot of torment."

He said then that he considered Bowen the type of person who could help his program recover from past controversies. "Let's get guys like that, who are very humble, but confident in their abilities," he said, describing what attracted him to Bowen. "When adversity hits you really gotta make sure it doesn't affect moving forward. You learn from the past. You don't live in it."

Pitino filed two lawsuits. The first was against the University of Louisville Athletic Association, a related entity of the school that was technically his employer, claiming that his dismissal violated the terms of his contract. He had been fired "for cause," it said, without legitimate cause. It asks: If Pitino was involved in payoffs or arranging for them, why isn't his voice caught on the wiretaps and why isn't he captured on video in any of the meetings?

The lawsuit summarized the federal criminal case—that Adidas allegedly had conspired to funnel money to the families of high school players to Adidas-sponsored schools—and noted that one of those named, Bowen, had in fact enrolled at Louisville. But it said that he had nothing to do with any exchanges of money. "Coach Pitino had no part—active, passive, or through willful ignorance—in the conspiracy described in the Complaint," the suit said. "Coach Pitino never has had any part . . . in any effort . . . to pay any recruit, or any family member of a recruit, or anyone else on a recruit's behalf, as an inducement to attend the University of Louisville."

Pitino's lawyer, Steve Pence, a former lieutenant governor of Kentucky, points out in the lawsuit that while Pitino's name comes up in conversations among Dawkins and other defendants, Pitino himself is not present on any of the recordings. The defendants "bragged" about influence with him they did not have, it says. A claim by Dawkins that he talked to Pitino and asked him to make a call to Jim Gatto in order to secure money from Adidas for Bowen "lacks all credibility" because if that conversation had taken place, it should have been captured on the wiretap of Dawkins's phone—and the government "surely would have said so."

The FBI, though, also has records of calls between Pitino and Gatto (though apparently not recordings of their conversations)—and in documents, the government alleges that Pitino agreed to ask the shoe company to provide more money for Dawkins. Pence has characterized the conversations as entirely innocent in nature. Pitino at one point said that the subject of at least one of the calls involved a dispute regarding an endorsement contract between Adidas and one of his former players, Terry Rozier, now of the Boston Celtics. (Rozier had worn Nikes in some games, and Pitino said he was interceding on his former player's behalf to prevent his Adidas contract from being canceled.)

Pitino's lawsuit argues that, as opposed to participating in schemes that violated NCAA rules, he was a stickler for running a clean program. "He drilled compliance into his coaches and assistants at every meeting," his complaint says. "He met with his coaches and assistants frequently and kept well informed about their activities."

Pitino did not ask for his job back. He sought "the full unpaid balance" of his contract—$35 million—or what he would have earned for coaching to the end date of his deal in June 2026.

Pitino's second lawsuit was filed against Adidas and is notable for its blunt language in describing the motivations of shoe companies in putting big dollars into college athletics. He profited from that money for many years. To the extent that his players were being turned into human billboards, it was to his benefit. Before Louisville signed its much more lucrative deal with Adidas in 2017, Pitino received 98 percent of the cash from the old contract, or approximately $1.5 million a year over the previous five years.

When athletic director Tom Jurich announced the new ten-year, $160 million extension, his emphasis was on the close relationship between the school and the company—a feeling of "family," as he put it. The apparel companies like to stress the performance advantages of their products—as if, for example, an Adidas shoe, jersey, or wristband might help eke out a victory over an inferiorly outfitted athlete at a Nike school. It is silly, of course, but it gives executives something to talk about other than their real strategies. In 2015, when Indiana extended its deal with Adidas, Chris McGuire, the company's senior director of sports marketing, said, "We've worked closely with the Hoosiers to bring our best and most innovative footwear, apparel, and accessories to all men's and women's sports. We've enjoyed a successful partnership with Indiana and look forward to continuing to collaborate to help their athletes perform at the highest level."

Pitino may be an imperfect and unlikely messenger, but his lawsuit cuts through all the corporate happy talk and gets to the crux of what the contracts are about. "It was and is in Adidas's interest to have the schools that Adidas outfits succeed, especially because high-profile television coverage of championship events would show athletes wearing Adidas products," his complaint reads. "It is likewise and was in Adidas's interest for top athletes to attend the schools that Adidas outfits, because that would increase the chance of those teams' success. And it was in Adidas's long-term interest to build relationships with recruits early in their careers to influence them to sign contracts with Adidas once they became professional athletes." The suit says that Adidas knew the NCAA rules but realized that "violating these regulations could benefit them financially."

The legal language does nothing to obscure the clear point being made: Adidas and the other apparel companies are in the business of pimping out athletes, as it might be said on the street. Throw some money their way. Dress them up, put them in front of the public, and reap the benefits.

In response, Adidas asked the judge to either dismiss Pitino's lawsuit or move it to arbitration. It refers to the FBI investigation and states, "Although Pitino claims he had no involvement with any conspiracy to direct payments to the basketball player's family, the criminal complaint includes allegations suggesting that he was both aware of and supported the scheme." An oddity of both of the lawsuits filed by Pitino is that they prominently reference the other recent scandal in the Louisville basketball program—the "Strippergate" episode. (The episode is repeatedly referred to as "the escort matter.")

You could argue that such behavior, taking place a short walk from Pitino's office and involving people under his supervision, does not reflect positively on him and would not work in his favor in any kind of legal battle. But his lawsuits take the opposite view: His lawyer reasons that Strippergate was so awful, so publicly humiliating and damaging that it would make him extra careful about risking another scandal. It is not the kind of logic you would be likely to hear in a criminal courtroom—a defense lawyer arguing, say, that his client has committed crimes in the past, so knowing the consequences, why would he chance it again?

Pitino, however, is portrayed as a coach who ran an otherwise rule-abiding program. "Adidas outrageously conspired to funnel money to a recruit or the family of a recruit," his lawyer wrote, without regard for how Pitino's "public and private standing and reputation hinged on him running a clean, proper and strictly compliant men's basketball program. This is particularly true in light of the recent, well-publicized matter resulting from an assistant coach's improper provision of escorts to University of Louisville men's basketball players and recruits." The lawsuit states that Pitino had a "reputation for honesty and integrity" that was tarnished by Adidas and seeks damages from the company for having "recklessly caused [him] emotional distress."

Pitino would begin to talk about coaching again, and his name was linked to several possible jobs, including a couple in the NBA—a measure of respect for his coaching acumen. When the

2018 season began, he would be sixty-six years old and nearly two decades past his last time on the sideline of an NBA game, but no knowledgeable basketball person doubted his ability to make any team, pro or college, better.

When we talked in January, he was still subdued. He used the word "assassinated" or "assassination" no less than five times. When I asked about his future, he replied, "I haven't even thought about it. There's some mornings I don't even feel like fighting anymore. I've been assassinated."

He had long maintained a cordial relationship with journalists, who enjoyed his banter, but he complained about the coverage of him in the press. "I don't have it out for the media," he said. "But the media today has a different culture. It's a no-win battle. . . . Years ago, they wanted the facts, now everybody wants to be first. Ask any of my assistant coaches who worked for me—it was impossible for me to give anybody five dollars. I have never given anything illegal to any athlete at any time."

He brought up the two big scandals in his past. He didn't see why people continued to blame him for the parties in the basketball dorm featuring the escorts—or how he could possibly have known what was taking place. High school recruits stayed overnight when they came for their campus visits, and he would see them at breakfast. What coach would have asked them if they had met any strippers the previous night? He had no reason to suspect it.

With one exception—his own humiliation following a night in a Louisville restaurant—everything bad that had happened to him in Louisville was the fault of others. People he hired didn't listen to him. They did things he never could have imagined. He repeated what has become a stock line when something has gone wrong in his program: "All I can say is, I taught them to do the right thing."

CHAPTER ELEVEN

THE CHARDONNAY CROWD

E very city in the United States that is not New York has an
inferiority complex of some kind. Chicagoans, for all the
attributes of their city, worry that it is seen as provincial.
Philadelphia is ninety miles from New York, but its inhabitants are
acutely aware that it will never be New York. (They celebrate the
trickle of New Yorkers who are drawn to Philly by word of it being
"the new Brooklyn.") Angelenos fret over a perceived lack of intel-
lectual heft, and there are actually people in San Francisco who
obsess over the inability of any bakery in their city to make a proper
bagel.

A regional city like Louisville generally just wants to be noticed,
to register in some small way on the national consciousness, and

that is the slice of its psyche that Tom Jurich so brilliantly converted into money. It mattered that the university takes its name from the city. There are just a handful of other such universities playing major sports, and most of them, unlike Louisville, compete with pro teams for attention. When the Cardinals played football on Tuesday nights, that was *Louisville* on national TV. When Pitino's kids won their national title, their jerseys said *Louisville*. When people referred to "the 'Ville," they were talking not just about the school, but the city. "This community, the U. of L., its psyche, its pride, and its self-confidence, are interlocked," Abramson, the former mayor, said. "You can't separate it."

When Jurich arrived in 1997, construction of Papa John's Cardinal Stadium was already under way. Even as it was still being completed, he began raising an additional $75 million to add yet more seats and luxury boxes. He raised $11.6 million for a natatorium. For a rowing center: $2.65 million. A baseball stadium, and later its expansion: $11.3 million. Soccer: $18.5 million. The purchase of a golf course and renovation of its grounds: $11.3 million. An indoor golf practice facility: $850,000. Various other practice facilities: at least $21 million. A tutoring center for athletes: $18.5 million. For Billy Minardi Hall, the basketball dormitory named for Pitino's late brother-in-law: $4.5 million.

People in Louisville who did not know they were fans of lacrosse or swimming or soccer found themselves taking pride in the university's status as an all-around sports power. They gave generously. Those who parted with millions got their names on the buildings.

Jurich's daughters were both athletes—high-achieving field hockey players in high school who were recruited, on merit, to Louisville. He raised tens of millions of dollars for the women's teams not just to get Louisville out of noncompliance with Title IX regulations—and to allow it to conference-jump all the way into the prestigious ACC—but, to his credit, because he deeply believed in the value of women's sports. True to form, he did also see it in terms of money. He knew that few if any of his female athletes would get rich in professional sports, but he believed that a background in competitive athletics would help women in the business world— and he hoped that some of them would become wealthy enough to become donors to the university and its athletic department. When he was raising money for their teams, that was all part of his pitch.

The current football stadium is one of the best-appointed in the NCAA. Among its amenities is the Brown and Williamson Club— twenty-eight luxury suites stretching the length of the football field. The club takes its name from the tobacco company, manufacturers of Lucky Strikes and Pall Mall, among other brands, that was once headquartered in Louisville and is now a division of RJ Reynolds.

The stadium is undergoing yet another expensive renovation. Before he was fired, Jurich began raising an additional $63 million to close off the north end zone—the stadium had been a horseshoe— and add more premium seating. (The project is still at least $20 million short.) The new expansion, the university announced in 2015, will include club seats adjacent to "a gathering area [with] an exclusive view to the players, who will be running on to the gridiron from a middle-of-the-field level entrance after exiting the football complex through a tunnel."

The concept of the field-level suites, taken from Dallas Cowboys owner Jerry Jones, was its own bit of genius. There are strict rules about how universities can individually market their NCAA student-athletes. But here, Jurich created an exclusive seating area where fans will pay to be able to literally reach out and touch their favorite players as they come on and off the field. It is called the Adidas Three Stripe Zone, after the three angled stripes on the company's logo, and its marketing promises a "one of a kind experience" in which fans will get "close-up access at the team runout."

In all, Jurich raised about $280 million in construction funds, mostly for the stadiums, ballparks, arenas, and state-of-the-art practice facilities along Floyd Street—the eastern edge of campus the university calls its "front porch." The money came mostly from local donors, many of them trustees. But the biggest givers were not by and large alumni; they were fans of Louisville sports.

The total does not include the $238 million it took to build the KFC Yum! Center. That was public money, from taxpayers, but the favorable lease extended to the university—an "astonishingly lopsided" agreement, Bloomberg News called it—represented Jurich's biggest coup. It was a bad deal for the city but a great one for Louisville athletics.

The Yum Center, which seats more than 22,000 for basketball, features seventy-two luxury suites that rent for between $75,000 and $92,000 each. Some courtside seats go for as much as $15,000 each for the season—or about $750 a game. Even though the university did not pay to build the arena, the lease provides that it receives 88 percent of premium seat revenue, 97 percent of suite sales, and half of the take from concessions. (That includes receipts from beer and wine, as well as from hard liquor, which is not sold in most college arenas.) "It's unusual for an arena to be run by the tenant, but the U. of L. has almost total control of Yum Center," one of the building's concessionaires said. "It was built for them and they call the shots."

The lease terms and the popularity of Pitino's teams, which

regularly sold out their games, made Louisville's program far and away the most profitable in college basketball. Its $45.6 million in revenue in 2017 was $15 million more than Duke, the second-highest program, which does not have luxury boxes at its on-campus Cameron Indoor Stadium. Neither does Rupp Arena, where the University of Kentucky in most recent seasons has led college basketball in attendance. The big money in college sports, as in pro sports, is at the upper end of the market.

Yum Center was built to NBA specifications, including a full-sized practice court inside the building. The Louisville metropolitan area is bigger than New Orleans and Salt Lake City, which have NBA franchises, and about the same size as two other NBA cities, Oklahoma City and Memphis. The flourishes added at the Yum Center to attract the NBA added tens of millions of dollars to what was already an expensive project, and have contributed to the arena sinking under the weight of its debt.

Political and business leaders in Louisville believed they had a strong chance of attracting the NBA franchise that ultimately moved from Charlotte and became the New Orleans Pelicans. Jurich, however, not only succeeded in giving fans a pro-like experience, but he also either directly used his influence to keep an NBA team out of Louisville, or—by establishing the university as Yum's primary tenant, meaning it had its choice of dates during basketball season—made it untenable for an NBA team.

There already was a "pro" team in Louisville—Pitino's squad. If an NBA team had come into Louisville, the university would have had to share the arena and compete for the loyalty of the corporations and wealthy individuals who can afford suites and luxury seating. Without an NBA team, the Cardinals had that market all to themselves.

Jurich denied that he ever actively opposed an NBA team coming into the market. "I was never asked about it, so I couldn't say no," he said. Others have different recollections. Said Abramson, who was mayor during the planning and construction of the arena, "Jurich and Pitino made it very clear that they had no interest in sharing the Yum Center with an NBA team." David Stern, the NBA commissioner at the time, told Bloomberg that he remembered thinking when Louisville came up as a possible destination for a franchise, "If Rick Pitino doesn't want us there, why are we going there?"

Jonathan Blue, the former trustee, and the managing director of an equity firm in Louisville, was a strong supporter of Jurich's and opposed his firing. But he disagreed with him about an NBA franchise. "They are single-handedly responsible for us not having an NBA team," he said, referring to Jurich and Pitino. "I was for it. An NBA team puts a city on the map more than a great college basketball team is ever going to do. It would have solidified the success of the arena.

"But Jurich was raising money for two expansions of the football stadium, soccer facilities, baseball. It went on and on and there's only so much disposable income. He didn't want to compete over the dollars, the media buy, or the attention. Once the NBA deal was dead, we had to deal with what we had left. It was brilliant business on Jurich's part, but it had implications for the city."

The Yum Center became a burden to the city even before it opened. The bonds for its construction were supposed to be largely paid off from taxes thrown off by increased commercial activity downtown, spurred by the arena. That did not happen, in part because of the recession of 2008, which hit as it was still being constructed. But the ongoing problem was that the deal disadvantaged the city.

A 2017 state audit said that since the 2010 opening of Yum, the arena authority "has faltered badly" while the finances of the Louisville athletic department "dramatically improved." In the previous year, the audit said, the university earned $5.9 million for suite rentals while just $200,000 went to the city. The split from premium seats was $7 million to the U. of L. and $932,000 to the city.

The arena authority managed to restructure the debt and get the university to agree to contribute about $2.4 million more each year—but by extending the bond payments as far into the future as 2054 (they had been set to expire in 2029), the public money expended on the project could reach $1 billion.

The arena's troubles were the source of rare bipartisan agreement among politicians. A Republican in the state legislature called the contract "an unmitigated fleecing of taxpayers." A Democrat said it was another example that "there's a lot at University of Louisville that has smelled in recent years."

A s U. of L. sports got bigger and ever more of a rallying point, they upended the city's social structure. There was a sense in town that to be a donor to the athletic department—and to mix with others in the suites and premium seating areas at the football and basketball games—was helpful to whatever other aspirations one might have. "If you played in Jurich's pool," as one city leader put it, "you elevated yourself."

Jurich made $5.35 million in total compensation in 2016, some of which came from the University of Louisville Foundation, which manages the endowment. Dozens of people in the athletic department made salaries well into the six figures, which is not unusual in the NCAA. The high end of compensation is generally set by the men's basketball coach and the head football coach (at Louisville, Pitino was making $7.8 million; Bobby Petrino makes almost $5 million, and $5.5 million with bonuses, but others are also well compensated. Louisville's women's basketball coach makes $1.15 million; its baseball coach, $1 million; its men's soccer coach, $330,000; its women's volleyball coach, $200,000.

The university, for Jurich, was a family affair. His son Mark came back to the university after five years of playing minor-league baseball and worked as a fund-raiser for the athletic department. He stayed on after his father left but was fired several months later. His daughter Haley worked as an Adidas brand communication manager in Louisville.

College sports plays by its own special rules. Nepotism is so common that it mostly goes unremarked upon. Bobby Petrino's son Nick is the quarterbacks coach on his staff. (According to his bio on the athletics website, Nick has never had any coaching jobs except on his father's staff, following him from Arkansas to Western Kentucky to Louisville.) Petrino's son-in-law L. D. Scott is also on his staff, serving as defensive line coach. Between them, they make more than $500,000 a year. In January 2018, he hired *another* son-in-law, leaving him with three family members on his ten-man coaching staff.

Rick Pitino's son, the current head coach at Minnesota, spent three years on his father's staff at Louisville, one of them as associate head coach. Keep in mind that these are jobs at a state-funded institution, not a family business. The coaches' kids might be great at their jobs, but it's hard to think of other publicly funded entities where chief executives can lard their leadership teams with family members.

What Jurich built, with the help of the coaching acumen and charisma of Pitino, is a paradigm of big-time NCAA sports—a demonstration project of its benefits and dangers. Powerhouse sports programs often serve as a unifying force, but they are ultra-aggressive, gobbling up territory as they advance. They redefine campus dialogue. Myth becomes fact. The way to build a better academic institution is through sports? Yes, sometimes, but Duke was a pretty good school before Coach K came along, and if you look at any list of top universities, most of them do not achieve in sports at Louisville's level, or even try.

Ramsey's physical improvements to the university and the buzz of the winning teams helped lift up important markers at Louis-ville, including what had been an abysmal graduation rate. (Studies show that students who enjoy a campus are more likely to do what it takes to stay there.) But by most evidence, the academic aspects of the U. of L. did not rise at anywhere near the same rates as its teams did. The U. of L. was ranked No. 165 by *U.S. News* in its 2018 guide to the nation's "best colleges and national universities"—between the University of California–Merced and Mississippi State. The J. B. Speed School of Engineering is generally considered the strongest of Louisville's academic offerings; it was ranked 125th among undergraduate engineering programs by *U.S. News*.

Academic departments are not all intended as profit centers. An English department, to give one example, may turn out some liter-ature scholars, but it is also tasked with teaching future scientists and engineers how to write effectively. Humanities courses can serve to round out students who move on to practical careers, or at least that's the hope. By its nature, sports engenders linear thinking. Wins and losses. Hits and errors. Yards gained. The assists-to-turnovers ratio. It all goes on the stat sheet and players are held individually accountable.

When challenged about the centrality of athletics on campus, Jurich argued that everyone on campus should pull their own weight, just as the athletic department did—and as any division in a corporate structure must. It is the way he understood the world. "They couldn't have gone out and raised money?" he said in an *ESPN The Magazine* piece, in response to criticism that his salary alone was more than the budgets of the biology, English, history, and math departments. "Why is it I'm accountable for everything and all we've done is been successful? But these other people get a free pass? If I was a humanities professor, do you think I'd sit there and say, 'Man, I can't get it done, poor me'? I'd never say that. I'd go find a way to get it done. You know what? Those schools have alumni too. Those schools have very rich graduates too. Nobody handed me anything when I walked into this place. Nobody. It was quite the contrary."

Jurich could be genial and charming, and when he was not feeling challenged he was easy to be around. It's a big part of what made him so effective. But if you hit him, he hit you right back. If he had the upper hand in a negotiation, he used it. One reason why Pitino respected him is that he recognized Jurich as a fellow competitor. In 2016, when the criticisms of the arena lease got louder, Jurich responded, accurately, that no one had put a gun to the city's head and forced it to make the deal. He said he was "baited" downtown and would always have preferred an on-campus arena.

In a radio interview, he said that if political leaders did not feel the arrangement was fair, the sides could unwind the lease and the Cardinals would just build in south Louisville along Floyd Street in sight of the NFL-quality football stadium. It would be the newest and maybe the grandest addition to his sports complex.

That was probably not realistic. Even Jurich would have struggled to raise money in a city that he had just left with a huge white elephant—which is what the Yum Center would have become without Cardinals basketball. (It was in bad enough shape with it.)

But he insisted that this was the best solution, even after the radio host said he thought it would hurt the city. "Well, I think we should," he said. "I don't think we're wanted down there, so I think we should."

To speak out or even raise a concern about Louisville athletics was like standing in front of a moving tank. Not everyone was willing. There were dissenters, but it was difficult for them.

Emily Bingham is not someone who agrees to sit obediently and keep quiet. Her forthright nature is something she comes by honestly: She is a scion of the Binghams of Louisville, one of the South's storied families ("the Kennedys of inner America," *Vanity Fair* magazine once called them) and the owners, from 1937 to 1986, of the *Louisville Courier-Journal*. The Binghams' politics are liberal, and their newspaper reported aggressively. "There was always a *Courier-Journal* reporter around to challenge the timber cutters, the strip miners, the polluters, the corrupt," John Ed Pearce, a forty-year veteran of the paper, said after a bitter family feud led to the sale of the paper to the Gannett chain.

Barry Bingham Jr., Emily's father and the longtime *Courier-Journal* publisher, was not a big sports fan, though he knew that sports coverage sold newspapers. He had some quirks. One was that he did not like corporate references seeping onto the sports pages, and so he ordered his writers to use other names for such events as the Marlboro Cup horse race and the Kemper Open golf tournament.

In 2013, Emily Bingham was appointed by Kentucky's then governor, Steve Beshear, to the University of Louisville's board of trustees. She has a Ph.D. in history from the University of North Carolina, has taught at several universities, was an author of some note, and was the only academic on the board not employed by the university. Bingham joined a couple of other trustees who had been persuaded to join by Beshear and Abramson, who had become the state's lieutenant governor. Both of the politicians are Democrats, as were Bingham and her small, like-minded faction on the trustees board, but the divide was more cultural than political.

U. of L. sports was the plaything of Louisville's business class and, to a certain extent, of its new money as well. Bingham's cohorts were Steve Wilson, who had married into the Brown-Foreman bourbon family (Jack Daniel's, Woodford Reserve, and other brands), and Craig Greenberg, a lawyer and a partner with Wilson in 21C, a chain of boutique hotels in midsized cities with lobbies that double as art galleries. They were not opposed to sports, but they did not instinctively believe that sports should be the university's leading edge. "We tried to put people on the board who would ask questions," Abramson said.

Like all new trustees, Bingham was given an orientation, in which she was informed about the board's customs and ways of doing business. One important bit of guidance was that trustees should avoid asking any questions of substance at public meetings of the board, which were open to the press. The real discussions, she was told, take place in the president's box at football and men's basketball games, as everyone is wearing red, enjoying the buffet and open bar. "I thought, 'That's not going to work for me,'" she recalled. "I was pretty astonished." The atmosphere of cheering for the sports teams carried over into the boardroom. "You were either a cheerleader or an enemy," she said.

Ramsey, the university's president, was an economist whose career had been divided between teaching at five different universities and working in state government in Frankfort. He grew up in a hardscrabble part of south Louisville, as he liked reminding people, in a manner that could seem pointed, especially in contrast to the new trustees. He was appointed to lead the U. of L. in 2002, five years into Jurich's tenure, and as often happens with a long-serving CEO, he consolidated a great deal of power. He handpicked many of the trustees, and they were his loyalists and fans. In addition to serving as the school's president, Ramsey was president of the University of Louisville Foundation, which controlled the university's endowment.

Ramsey and Jurich both had forceful personalities and worked well together mostly by staying within their own spheres. They had what one associate of theirs called "a mutually beneficial détente." Jurich was a prodigious fund-raiser, and Ramsey was able to share in the credit for money he raised. When Jurich threw his loyalty behind coaches who came under fire, Ramsey did not interfere.

They both were paid high salaries—compensation that was more generous than their peers around the country, and was reflected in the university's bookkeeping in less than straightforward ways. That was a theme—hazy finances—that would later come out in a "forensic audit" of the university ordered by the state.

In 2015, Bingham and some others on the board began raising concerns about Ramsey's salary, and particularly the practice of paying him "gross-ups"—basically, paying his taxes for him.

Another trustee, Ron Butt, came to Ramsey's defense, comparing his performance guiding the university with the accomplishments of a superstar athlete. "How are you going to put a price tag on Michael Jordan if he comes to play for your team?" he said. "Are you going to pay him more than everybody else? Yeah. If for no other reason than intimidation. Jim is highly respected and sought after."

When a vote of no confidence in Ramsey came up for a vote, and narrowly failed, the board's president, Robert Hughes, a doctor in Murray, Kentucky, composed a diatribe against the dissident trustees. The forum he chose was a blog that followed U. of L. sports called Card Game. "These problems of the Board of Trustees began in 2013 with a core group from a zip code in the east end," he wrote, making it clear that he felt his opponents were effete. "This group has been relentless in pushing forward with incessant negatives and attempts to micromanage the university. I haven't seen anything positive from them since they were added to the board; they have added nothing constructive to the debate or to the life of the university."

In July 2015, after the Katina Powell revelations broke, Emily Bingham wrote a column for the *Courier-Journal*. Its unsparing tone signaled that her frustration had finally boiled over. "A core responsibility of a board is employing and paying its leaders, yet we have been lied to about the president's compensation," she wrote. "We cannot move forward without honesty from the leader we employ." She made reference to "countless rumors of self-dealing" and "conflicts of interest," a lack of "complete information," and a "culture of theft."

She then took on the athletic program, and in particular, the university's venerated head coach. "In a basketball program already embarrassed by the sexual misconduct of its coach, egregious alleged sexual misconduct by employees and players was never met with clear, forceful condemnation from the president. Waiting for years for NCAA judgment is unacceptable. We cannot move forward with leaders whose moral compass on these issues is not clear."

This was too much for Pitino. It did not seem to register—or certainly not to matter to him—that the criticism was coming from a person with some history and standing in Louisville. If he knew anything about Bingham or her family, he did not betray it. What he knew was that she was not on his team. In a radio interview, he referred to her repeatedly as "that lady," as if Bingham were a nobody taken off the streets and elevated to the board of trustees.

In a blog post, he retreated to his usual defense when he felt challenged. He could not be judged by mortals because God was already judging him. "That trustee would be better served trying to get a dysfunctional board on some form of a team," he wrote. "I'll make a suggestion to the person I have not met: Let God judge and get out of your glass house."

Larry Benz, then chairman of the board, came to Pitino's defense. "We join our athletic director, Tom Jurich, in our complete support of him."

An emphasis on athletics at a university—which always equates to the revenue sports of football and men's basketball—by its very nature tilts the conversation toward men. They know the sports intimately. They read the recruiting blogs. They have the strong opinions on coaching strategies, and if an official makes a poor call during a game, they are the ones most likely to shout their displeasure—even if they are in the president's box and splash their bourbon while doing so. (The bar's open; you can always get a refill.)

At its most extreme, the focus on sports boils over into misogyny.

Bingham got hate emails from Louisville sports fans, some of them crude in nature. Feeling under siege, she privately told Pitino she regretted her remarks—and, in fact, she had meant to direct her fire more at Ramsey and to issues involving the governance of the university. The *Courier-Journal* considered her communication with the basketball coach worthy of a story, headlining it, "Bingham Apologizes to Pitino for Comments."

The unraveling of the Ramsey-Jurich-Pitino regime at Louisville occurred in stages. It was a slow-motion, chaotic drama that featured the daylighting of the university's tangled and troubling finances, which were, by design, nearly indecipherable. A new Kentucky governor in 2016 fired the university's entire board of trustees, was ordered to reinstate them by a judge, and then, after figuring out how to do it legally, fired them again and appointed a new board. Emily Bingham and her allies were among the board members replaced. At the same time, James Ramsey, the longtime president, was swept out after Governor Matt Bevin requested and received his resignation.

A constant throughout all the twists and turns was the backbiting and backstabbing among people who were once allies. John Schnatter, the founder of Papa John's, was a key figure in the intrigue. Referred to by almost everyone in town as "Papa John," Schnatter lives in the Louisville suburb of Anchorage on an estate that makes Pitino's mansion on Indian Creek Island seem like a starter home. The main house is 40,000 square feet, not including the twenty-two-car underground garage. The sixteen-acre grounds include man-made ponds and a three-hole golf course. ("Who would've imagined pizza could build this?" Mitt Romney marveled at a political fund-raiser Schnatter hosted for him. "This is really something. Don't you love this country?")

Schnatter contributed an initial $5 million for the naming rights of Papa John's Cardinal Stadium, which some considered a bargain after the program soared to national prominence. But he had contributed millions in the intervening years and had never let on, at least publicly, that he was anything but a gung-ho booster of Jurich, Pitino, and Louisville sports. It was Schnatter who shuttled Jurich and other university officials to Dallas for a tour of AT&T Stadium, the Cowboys' football palace, in his private plane.

Schnatter was a member of the newest iteration of the board of trustees, and in the spring of 2017, he abruptly went on a diatribe against the athletic department. "The athletics thing scares me," he said at a board meeting. "Until you fix athletics, you cannot fix this university."

The website Insider Louisville, which closely covers the city and university, asked, "What's Papa Cooking?" There were many theories around town. One had to do with an argument that Schnatter and Pitino had in the parking lot at Valhalla, a golf club where they both belonged, supposedly over one of them not wanting to pay on a bet.

When anyone took a shot at Pitino, or he felt they had, he would not say their name. That's how Emily Bingham earned the sobriquet "that lady." After Schnatter turned on him and Louisville sports, Pitino henceforth referred to him as "the pizza guy." Sometimes he amended that and just called him "pizza boy."

Whatever Schnatter's motivations were—and however unlikely it was that the right-wing pizza magnate would end up on the side of Emily Bingham and her friends—he was not wrong to be alarmed about the state of affairs at the U. of L. (Schnatter is close with prominent conservative donors Charles and David Koch, and has combined with them to fund free enterprise institutes at both Louisville and the University of Kentucky.) His swings were big and wild at times, but mostly on point. He asked why the football stadium was being expanded yet again while attendance at games was falling. He said there was a "perception problem" with big spending for sports while faculty salaries were stagnant. He shifted his giving from athletics to academics and was not among the donors to the latest enhancements of Papa John's Cardinal Stadium.

In June 2017, a few months after Schnatter went public with his criticism—and three months before the FBI's investigation of college basketball brought down Rick Pitino and Tom Jurich—a long-awaited forensic audit of the university, ordered by the state, was completed. It revealed a situation at the U. of L. that, in the current vernacular, could best be described as a shit show.

The audit was dense and not easy to digest, but its conclusions were not complicated: The university was like a household living beyond its means. Its ambitions and taste for luxury exceeded its available resources. To make ends meet, it was dipping into its endowment to cover a range of expenditures, including operating expenses and salaries, and members of the administration had gone to great lengths to conceal some of the most questionable spending.

What most everyone had considered a golden age for the University of Louisville suddenly looked a lot different. When the audit's findings were made public, Greg Postel, the interim president, said, "This report should answer many questions about the past and close the door on a sad chapter in the university's history."

The audit's main finding was that up to 10 percent of the university's $790 million endowment had been liquidated and that the university was dipping into it at a rate that could eventually exhaust the whole fund. Some of the money went to questionable real estate endeavors and to investments in poorly performing start-up companies.

The athletic department featured prominently in the report. The president's office was purchasing about $800,000 in season tickets annually for football and men's basketball games and using endowment funds to do so. The "ticket purchases contributed to the ULF [University of Louisville Foundation] liquidation of pool assets," the report said, meaning the spending down of its endowment. Some of the seats were given as gifts to prospective donors. The president's office supposedly sold some of them, but there were no records of the sales or indications that they ever brought in any money.

Endowment funds were used to buy a golf course for the university's men's and women's teams. They were used to pay portions of Jurich's deferred compensation, and to fund his "gross-ups"—the paying of his taxes. The foundation had engaged in some complex transactions with the University of Louisville Athletic Association (the funding arm of the athletic department) in which it seemed to get the short end of the deal. In one such case, the report said, "the foundation spent $15.1 million on ULAA's behalf for which it received $11.6 million in consideration."

The questionable spending on sports was part of a larger, university-wide trend. The auditors uncovered a 2012 memo from the foundation's investment advisor warning that if the foundation continued its current practices, "There is a non-trivial chance that the endowment could cease to exist within the next 20 years."

Most of the nearly three-hundred-page document was dry, as one would expect in a report prepared by accountants and dealing with intricate financial machinations, but there were comic passages having to do with efforts to keep certain transactions and expenditures out of public view. An assistant to Ramsey wrote the foundation's lawyer about some of the deferred compensation deals. "How can we keep these . . . from being subject to ORR?"—meaning open records requests. "I am certain Dr. Ramsey does not want any of these to end up in the hands of the C-J [*Louisville Courier-Journal*]." In her emails, she expressed concerns that the limited liability companies, or LLCs, created to pay certain expenditures might be too easily discovered by reporters and considered changing them "into something more obscure that would be difficult to find."

One such LLC is named Minerva. She proposed taking most of the vowels out of its name, and wrote, "We all need to worry. . . . We should try to find something that all of us can remember. What about MNRVA.LLC?"

The foundation lawyer, apparently unconvinced that excising the vowels was advisable (or, alternatively, that it provided the sufficient subterfuge), wanted to give it more thought. He responded, "Let's noodle on it."

After the audit was released, a story in the online edition of the *Courier-Journal* was headlined, "Audit Vindicates Former U of L Trustees Once Derided as 'Elitist' and 'the Chardonnay Crowd.'"

There was a strong sense that after a couple of decades on the rise, the university had embarrassed itself, and it went beyond the audit. The previous year, pictures had emerged from a Mexican-themed Halloween party hosted by Ramsey for his staff. He was dressed in a multicolored poncho and sombrero, and others were similarly attired, with some of them also wearing fake mustaches.

The photos harked back to an earlier era at U. of L., when such a dumb party idea might have seemed in keeping with its down-market image. Nobody would have cared—or for that matter, even noticed. But the new U. of L. had higher aspirations, and the photos were not in accordance with them. The university apologized in a statement addressed to "Hispanic/Latino Faculty, Staff and Students," and pledged to "institute immediate training on diversity and racial equality issues." (And even that was embarrassing. Did U. of L. administrators really need diversity training to know not to dress up as fake Mexicans?)

A far more serious problem than bad publicity over the Halloween party was that the U. of L.'s accrediting body, the Southern Association of Colleges and Schools, took the extraordinary step of placing it on probation in January 2017. The association made a judgment that the university was in chaos. The move by Governor Bevin to fire the trustees—and to ask for the resignation of Ramsey—was particularly disturbing to the accrediting board, which was alarmed that the institution was being run by a political figure rather than a board of trustees and its academic leadership.

It said that if the U. of L. did not come into compliance, "removal from membership" was an option—which would have made its diplomas worthless. No one really thought that that extreme measure would take place—and the probation was lifted twelve months later—but still, to be sanctioned by its accreditor was a terrible mark against the institution. The release of the audit was another. Three months after that, in the fall of 2017, the FBI announced its charges, and Pitino and Jurich were put on leave, then fired.

The *Chronicle of Higher Education* wrote, "The last 24 months have seen a seemingly nonstop flood of abysmal headlines for the

University of Louisville. It's endured multiple investigations of several stripes, it's faced an intense vacuum of leadership, and its very accreditation seems under threat. The news on Wednesday—that the basketball coach, Rick Pitino, and the athletic director, Tom Jurich, had been placed on administrative leave after another high-profile scandal—was just the cherry on top."

Jurich gave Louisville, the city and the school, more than it ever expected. The front porch on Floyd Street. Entry into the blue-blood Atlantic Coast Conference. The sense of being a pro town even without a professional franchise. Everything was tops, even the dance team, the Ladybirds, champions of the National Cheerleading Association in nine of the last ten years and three-time winners of the Hip Hop national title. They are not an NCAA sport, but he took them in under the umbrella of his athletic department because they represented excellence.

There is a great deal of support left for Jurich in Louisville—a sense that he pulled off some kind of miracle and that without him things will return to normal. Jim Patterson, a big donor whose name is on the baseball stadium (he contributed $3 million of the $11.2 million cost), urged interim president Greg Postel to spare Jurich after the recruiting scandal hit. "We are flying at 40,000 feet," he wrote to him. "Does it make sense to turn the engines off now?" Another donor, Max Baumgardner, an eighty-eight-year-old former pilot who made a fortune as an investor, revoked his $6.3 million bequest to U. of L. athletics and redirected the money elsewhere in the university, including to a program in the school of music (the Max Baumgardner Endowed Fund for Excellence in Jazz Studies).

There was an absurd aspect to the letter sent to Jurich informing him he was fired. It made it seem like the university, two decades into his tenure, had just discovered the nature of his management style. The letter from Postel to Jurich said that he had engaged in "willful misconduct," brought disrepute to the university, and engaged in "divisive leadership, unprofessional conduct, and a lack of collegiality best characterized as intimidation and bullying that extends from the student government to the university's senior leadership." (The letter informing Pitino of his dismissal had the same quality. "This notice arises out of your conduct over a period of years," it said, as if that had just come to their attention.)

One element of Jurich's alleged misconduct was that he did not properly supervise coaches, but everyone in town knew about his unwavering loyalty to his coaches—and not just the famous ones like Pitino. In 2013, the *Courier-Journal* reported on a women's lacrosse coach described as "an abusive taskmaster" who ran her team amid a culture of fear. Among the allegations against her was that she ordered a player with a torn anterior cruciate ligament in her knee to do 250 push-ups in an airport terminal as punishment, kicked another player off the team on a road trip and left her behind, and told two teammates to sign a contract pledging they would no longer speak to each other. The athletic department's spokesman responded after the story that there was "no next step planned" for the coach, and she stayed on for another four years. She was dismissed about a month after Jurich left.

In May 2018, the university changed course and settled with Jurich. It gave him $7.2 million, plus medical coverage and twenty years of prime tickets to U. of L. football and men's basketball games. It retreated from the position that he had been fired for cause and said he had retired.

In Steamboat Springs, before the agreement, Jurich talked about his sense of feeling betrayed. Three of his children remained in Louisville. His son Mark, whom he considered "the best young fund-raiser in the NCAA," had recently been dismissed from his job in Louisville's athletic department. A two-time all-American baseball player at Louisville, he was told he was not welcome to attend baseball games at Patterson Stadium, according to Jurich.

Tom Jurich worked extraordinarily long hours—there were really no waking hours that he was not working—because wherever he went, he was representing and selling the U. of L. He figured that even with his high salary, the university got a bargain. When he started at Louisville, the entire budget of the athletic department was about $14 million. By the time he left, it had reached $104.5 million.

"I was a B student, but I understand people," he said. "They all knew that I thought big. That's what they hired me to do. Nobody, the whole time I was there, ever expressed to me—sports is getting too big. How could I have known? I did what they hired me to do. I gave them what they wanted."

In contrast to Jurich, Rick Pitino thoroughly wore out his welcome in Louisville. Fans who had taken great pleasure from his teams, and who delighted in his swagger and wit, knew he had to go. Even his close friends used the phrase "third strike." People were tired of him.

The only one who did not realize it was Pitino himself. He insisted that he knew nothing about any side deals or money changing hands relating to the recruitment of Brian Bowen Jr.—just as he had known nothing about the escorts in the basketball dorm over the course of four years. He was an innocent. Forty years after he entered the fraternity of college basketball coaching, things still happened that were invisible to him, that he could not even imagine.

He blamed the escorts scandal solely on the staff member who set up the parties. "Did one person do some scurrilous things? I believe so," he said. "He knew better and was taught better by his parents and me." After news broke of the federal government's recruiting investigation and Louisville's featured role in it, he talked about all the great assistant coaches he had hired—and his utter bewilderment over what his young assistant coach Jordan Fair could have been up to in the hotel-room meeting with Christian Dawkins. "I'm not going to hang him out to dry," he said. "Whatever he did, it was a wrong move."

Living in Florida, with no job for the first time in his adult life, Pitino was college basketball's King Lear. Fuming and petulant, he failed to grasp that it didn't matter anymore what he did or did or did not know. Two catastrophic scandals had occurred on his watch, and they followed his own personal humiliation—the one-nighter with Karen Sypher, and his narration of it, in excruciating detail, under oath in federal court. No one, not even Rick Pitino, was going to survive a third fiasco.

In March 2018, one of Pitino's thoroughbreds, Coach Rocks, won a big race in Florida that qualified her to run in the annual Kentucky Oaks, an event for fillies that takes place the day before the Kentucky Derby at Churchill Downs. "With a determined surge" down the stretch, *BloodHorse* magazine reported, "Coach Rocks achieved what many believed was a lost cause—she made it possible for Rick Pitino to win another championship in Louisville."

But Pitino said he had no intention of traveling to Louisville to watch the race. He put conditions on what could change his mind, as if the people of Kentucky were clamoring for his return and might meet his demands. The current chairman of the university's board of trustees, which he referred to as "the board of traitors," would have to step down. And the vice chairman. "I will not go," he said, without the retirements of "David Grissom [the board chair]— and the pizza guy."

CHAPTER TWELVE

THE SPOILS OF UNCOMPENSATED LABOR

Prosecutors filed new charges in April 2018 that tied two more major basketball schools to the scandal—North Carolina State, a member of the Atlantic Coast Conference, and Kansas, a perennial Final Four participant and three-time national champion. The superseding indictment, as it is called, sharpened the connection between the shoe companies and alleged bribes paid to induce recruits to attend certain schools.

Jim Gatto, the Adidas executive, along with an unnamed consultant for the company (and presumably a cooperating witness), funneled money to the father of a high school star to get him to enroll at N.C. State, an Adidas-sponsored school, according to the government. The player was not named, but the description of him—"widely regarded as the top recruit" in North Carolina in the class of 2016—and the details on when he formally committed indicate it was Dennis Smith Jr., who played a year for the Wolfpack and now is a member of the NBA's Dallas Mavericks.

Gatto and the consultant were also alleged to have paid two different recruits who signed with Adidas-sponsored Kansas. In the case of all three players—the two at Kansas and the one at North Carolina State—the money was drawn from Adidas by Gatto and his cohort, paid to the accounts of the nonprofit AAU programs, and then redirected to the players' parents or guardians. In "sham invoices," as prosecutors described them, the payments were labeled as "travel expenses," "tournament fees," or "tournament activation fees." Gatto and his colleague were said to be working with Christian Dawkins and Merl Code to get the money to the families. Prosecutors said that the mother of one of the Kansas recruits was "personally delivered" a payment on October 31, 2016, in a New York hotel room—$30,000, in cash.

Notably, money paid to one of the Kansas recruits was needed to get him "out from under" a deal he had made with a rival shoe company—one that had already paid his family in order to direct him to one of their sponsored schools. Published reports said the rival athletic company was Under Armour. That, along with subpoenas reportedly served seeking information on Nike's grassroots program, further fueled suspicions that federal investigators will move on to the other shoe companies.

What, if any, of the activities described by the prosecution amount to federal crimes must still be determined, but no matter what, the government's case, if viewed in a different way—solely as a narrative that exposes the real deal of what takes place on the recruiting circuit—is thoroughly convincing and dovetails with long-held suspicions. The payoffs. The heedless exploitation of young athletes. The mélange of shady characters. The use of AAU teams as conduits for payoffs—essentially, pass-throughs in a money-laundering scheme. It all rings true. There are no insiders—coaches, parents, athletic directors, agents, recruiting gurus, NBA scouts—who can honestly express any shock.

When news broke of the arrests in the fall of 2017, prominent college coaches attempted to walk a fine line between not wanting to seem naïve (of course they knew some bad things took place out on the recruiting trail!) and not seeming to have direct knowledge of wrongdoing. "Any coach in this business that tries to act like there weren't some shenanigans going on . . . they're not being honest with you," said Frank Martin, the head coach at South Carolina.

Martin led his team to the Final Four in 2017 and is widely admired for his no-nonsense, streetwise manner. He once worked as a bouncer at a nightclub, and he came up from the bottom in the coaching profession, getting his first head coaching job at a high school in Miami only after eight years running the junior varsity. One of Martin's former assistants at South Carolina, Lamont Evans, is among those charged in the NCAA case, for alleged crimes that occurred at Oklahoma State after he left Martin's staff. Martin said he was "heartbroken" over Evans's arrest. When a reporter for the Associated Press asked him why, if he suspected that schools were breaking rules, he did not report it to the NCAA, he said, "There's no snitching within your family."

Other coaches expressed sadness and regret over what their business had become. The notion that they are "fishing in polluted waters"—recruiting kids who have become accustomed to receiving material benefits from middle school on up—was echoed by, among others, Duke's Mike Krzyzewski. "The grassroots culture of basketball has changed dramatically," he said. "We are not the only ones recruiting these youngsters. Talent is being recruited all the time in every shape and form."

Mark Fox, then at Georgia, was the rare coach who publicly alluded to having failed to sign players he coveted because some other school paid for them. "We've had some situations where we didn't get players because of that reason, and other teams have, too," he said, adding, "I'm disgusted with how people have treated our game. It's absolutely disgusting."

Fox's team had a disappointing year and Georgia fired him in March 2018, after nine seasons and just two appearances in the NCAA tournament. Rick Pitino was the only head coach fired in direct response to the federal case, and even that was related in part to his past transgressions.

Elsewhere, at programs with head coaches who were tied to the federal case, universities appeared to be trying to wait the crisis out. Arizona's Sean Miller, whose assistant coach, Book Richardson, was indicted in the scheme, sat out one game in late February after ESPN reported that he was caught on an FBI wiretap discussing a $100,000 payoff to a player. He disputed the report—other media outlets indicated it could be in error—and he was back coaching the next game. His university administration backed him, though provisionally, saying in a statement it would not rush to judgment but "continue to pursue every avenue of inquiry available to us" in the midst of an active federal investigation.

The uncertainty seemed to damage Miller's recruiting for a time, and there were concerns that Arizona might have to play the following season with just a handful of scholarship players. But memories are short in college sports, and optimism that issues will be papered over is usually rewarded. In the spring of 2018, the so-called late-signing period, Miller landed a six-foot-five guard from California by the name of Devonaire Doutrive. The sports site Arizona Desert Swarm predicted that "other dominoes would follow," and they did. Miller secured commitments from two other top prospects. He was back in the game, and it looked like his team would be just fine.

In October 2017, a month after prosecutors brought the charges, Mark Emmert, the NCAA's president, addressed the Knight Commission on Intercollegiate Athletics, which for a quarter century has been trying to figure out how to fix college sports. His plain language was rare for an NCAA official, and it indicated that he understood that the real victims were not his member schools, despite how the government shaped its case. "It's disgusting enough as it is," Emmert said in response to a question about where he thought the federal investigation was headed. "And we ought to recognize that we own that. That's part of us. When we see a coach, an assistant coach, making $200,000–$300,000 per year, taking a $10,000 bribe to throw some kid under the bus by steering him and his family to an irreputable financial advisor, you've got to be just sick to your stomach."

But he said he did not support decoupling sports from higher education, as is the case in most of the rest of the world, where professional sport is a career choice made by athletes in their mid- or late teens. They rarely go on to college. "When I travel around the world," Emmert said, "they all want to emulate our model, because they hate their model. And they all think that having education and athletics linked together is part of the secret sauce of America."

People may tell Emmert that, but the glaring contradiction of the NCAA is not the link between education and athletics—it's the conscription of young, ostensibly amateur athletes into a multibillion-dollar, profit-seeking sports-and-entertainment empire. You can say they get the benefit of a free education, but their sport is their job. They practice, lift weights, watch film, travel for games. It is true of scholarship athletes in all sports and at all levels at the scholarship-granting Division I level. (Several years ago, I gave a talk at a mid-sized Division I school. A player on the women's basketball team told me that she had hoped to major in nursing, but her coach told her she could not do the coursework and required labs and meet her team obligations, so she chose a less demanding major.)

The current model of big-time Division I sports is built on a foundation of utter hypocrisy: that participants in the two revenue sports are "student-athletes" and the NCAA and their schools equally value the student and athlete aspects of them. It's not true, and the athletes, their families, and any sentient fan knows it.

The two former players on the NCAA's Commission on College Basketball, the panel appointed after the indictments, David Robinson and Grant Hill are both members of basketball's Hall of Fame. They are estimable people, but neither is exactly representative of the kids emerging from the grassroots scene. Robinson is the son of a Navy engineer and the only NBA player ever to have graduated from the U.S. Naval Academy. Hill's father is a former NFL player and Yale graduate; his mother was Hillary Clinton's roommate at Wellesley. The chairwoman of the committee was Condoleezza Rice, an ardent sports fan and the secretary of state in the administration of President George W. Bush.

In its report, issued in April 2018, the commission demonstrated that it fully understood one of the NCAA's critical defects: It does not—and possibly cannot—enforce its most cherished rules. When it tries, it does so unequally and, it often seems, selectively. "No stakeholder supported the current system for handling high-stakes infractions," the report said. "Many informed us that when the U.S. Attorney's Office announced the charges that led to this commission, the reaction was that 'everyone knows' that these payments occur. That state of affairs, where the community knows of significant rule-breaking and yet the governance body lacks the power or will to investigate or act—breeds cynicism and contempt."

The committee proposed a range of sensible and possibly helpful reforms, chief among them doing away with the prohibition against players entering the NBA right from high school, the rule that ushered in the one-and-done era. It is the NBA's rule, however, part of its bargaining agreement with the players' association, and the league and union are the ones who would have to agree to make the change. Ending one-and-done would probably help a little. Perhaps a half dozen of the best high school prospects might opt to try to go right to the NBA, so there would be less frenzy around their recruiting—at least once the players' intentions were clear. But that would just take the top sliver of prospects off the market, and otherwise leave all the same temptations in place.

The panel recommended that high school players be allowed to consult with agents while still retaining their college eligibility, and be able to play in college if they declare their intention to play professionally but go undrafted by the NBA. As a way of lessening the influence of the shoe companies, it suggested that the NCAA sponsor its own camps or tournaments for high school prospects in July and decree that they are the only events that coaches can attend that month.

Their suggestions, however, are mostly around the edges and do not challenge the root cause of corruption: a structure that brings billions of dollars into the sport and richly rewards coaches and others within athletic departments. "We need to put the college back in college basketball," Rice said on the day the report was released. "Our focus has been to strengthen the collegiate model—not to move toward one that brings aspects of professionalism into the game."

Those are worthy goals, but her statement misses the point by defining "professionalism" only as money paid to players. If you market college games as entertainment and enter into billion-dollar deals with broadcast partners—and accept billions more from the very shoe companies said to be eating away at the integrity of your sport—the game is already plenty professionalized.

The eighty-page report has a great deal to say about cynicism in college sports, but it is silent on a major element of it: the high salaries paid to coaches and others in athletic departments. And all the profligate spending that is made possible by not paying the players. By not commenting, the commission missed an opportunity to point out the flip side of amateurism in college sport: coaches and administrators taking advantage of it to enrich themselves. Their silence implied they are fine with that.

There was one other glaring omission. The commission is highly critical of the apparel companies' practices on the grassroots circuit. They call them out by name—Nike, Adidas, and Under Armour—and identify them as "non-scholastic" influences that compromise athletes and their families. In the leagues they sponsor, the report notes, "many players and their families are accustomed to being paid before they attend college."

The commission wants the flow of money from the shoe companies to young players stopped. But what about the hundreds of millions of dollars flowing from those same three companies directly to NCAA schools? How can the shoe companies funneling relatively small sums of money to teenage players and their families be a corrupting influence—but those very same companies committing more than a billion dollars to NCAA universities, in very large increments to individual schools, not be of concern? Someone on the commission with a little more street sense, who could see it through the eyes of players, might have seen that contradiction and asked: Wait a second. How is it okay for the NCAA to take the money but not a kid or his family who might need it to pay the rent or keep the lights on?

In each case, the shoe money buys loyalty to the brand. The cost to players who take it is that they break NCAA rules. The cost to the universities is that they sell a part of their identity—an institution of higher learning becomes a "Nike school" or an "Adidas school." It pimps out its bookstore in branded gear. It mandates what shoes its athletes must wear, even if something else might fit better.

The members of the Commission on College Basketball may have believed they were thinking big, but their proposed fixes are small, and the scope of their inquiry was limited. The corrupting influences in college sports are not exterior to the system. The rot comes from the structure of college sport itself.

There is every reason to pay college football and men's basketball players. It has yet to happen not just because leaders of the NCAA stubbornly hold on to an outdated model. That may not even be the biggest reason at this point. The bigger stumbling block is that no one has come up with a plan to pay them that seems to make sense.

There are gender equity questions. Do you pay athletes on the women's teams, none of which are revenue sports? (The term is a misnomer and really should be "profit sports." Women's basketball teams in Division I generally charge admission to games, as do some other women's sports, and they benefit from TV money generated by their season-ending tournament. But their revenues do not exceed their expenses.)

Do you spread the money around and pay men's and women's lacrosse and soccer players? Gymnasts, fencers, and swimmers? Field hockey players? They benefit from the money thrown off by football and basketball, which largely fund their sports, but they also bear some of the burdens. The configuration of conferences, designed for maximum TV exposure and revenue in the major sports, increases the travel across all sports. To give one example, teams in the geographically scattered American Athletic Conference travel for games in a circuit that includes stops in Connecticut, Philadelphia, Wichita, Houston, and Orlando. Why, exactly? A college volleyball player could not get the same benefit from his or her sport by competing against rivals closer to home?

If you only pay the men in basketball and football, because they're the ones generating money, are they employees? Do you pay the five-star recruit more than the four-star? Can you fire the quarterback if he starts throwing too many interceptions? Cut his pay from his sophomore to junior years if you recruit a younger kid who becomes the first-string QB?

Once you start paying, what is the rationale for not paying what they are truly generating in the market? NBA and NFL players get roughly 50 percent of team revenues. If you paid that to football and basketball players at the top programs, they would make millions. Can you effectively coach a team of late-teen millionaires? Should there be a salary cap, or could Duke and Kentucky have tens of millions more to spend on players than Wichita State and Butler?

Is that model marketable—fans rooting for, say, a team from the University of Maryland, Baltimore County, whose players are making peanuts, in a March Madness game against Virginia of the powerful ACC? (A replay of the first No. 16 seed to defeat a No. 1 seed in the NCAA tournament, only this time it would be pros against amateurs.) And *should* it be marketable, or is that the whole problem to begin with—college sports casting itself as big-money entertainment?

What if you decide it's not a good idea to have eighteen-year-olds, just out of their parents' houses for the first time, drawing big paychecks, living in luxury and driving around campus in Bentleys—so you hold their money in escrow? But that seems awfully paternalistic. What if an athlete needs the money now to take care of a family living in poverty? Does the NCAA decide to what extent their standard of living should be raised? For example, you can pay the rent and keep the heat on (but show us the bills), but the house in the better neighborhood with the pool in the backyard has to wait?

One obvious fix is to allow NCAA athletes to earn money from their likenesses, through endorsements, or even autograph signing—if they have the market value that allows it. It could be like an off-campus job. (And probably an off-season one.) If their families needed money, it would be one way to provide it. If the NCAA really wants athletes to stay in school, it might eliminate one big reason for leaving—that a kid's family is broke and he is eager to help them out.

By not paying players, big athletic departments have tens of millions of dollars to spread around—the spoils of uncompensated labor. A study by the *Chronicle of Higher Education* found that less than 1 percent of it goes to academic programs. Most of it stays in the sports program, and a big chunk of that pays salaries that are almost insanely generous—and not just to the football and men's basketball coaches. It is not unusual for coaches in baseball, volleyball, swimming, and a whole range of other nonrevenue sports in the Power Five conferences to make $250,000 and up, and that's not including their car allowances, a range of other benefits, and their bonuses for winning championships.

Louisville is one of the best examples of how college sports executives choose to spend their largesse. In 2016, Tom Jurich gave Dan McDonnell, his baseball coach since 2007, a ten-year, $10.6-million contract extension. It was a raise of $325,000 a year. Its length gave him job security beyond any manager in Major League Baseball. Even more surprising, his annual salary is greater than that of several big-league managers.

McDonnell, who previously was an assistant coach at the Citadel and Ole Miss, said after his new deal was unveiled, "God has blessed this program." He added that he had not even had to ask for a raise. "Tom is not the type you have to knock on the door and ask for things. He's one step ahead." Said Jurich, "He's earned it with a capital 'E.'" After McDonnell left the press conference, he said, "I still think he's underpaid."

W ith all that has happened at Louisville, it would make sense for the school's leadership to take a year or two and reassess its approach to athletics. Not to shut everything down, but to reimagine its central place at the institution and to think about whether it might make sense for it to be a quieter, more modest, and less money-centered force.

But it's impossible. The beast must be fed. Attendance for football needs to be juiced back up to justify the expense of the latest expansion of the stadium. In Louisville's first post-Pitino year, the crowds at the Yum Center dropped sharply. That has to be fixed and the leaseholders of the suites must be coaxed to renew. There's a baseball coach to pay and a whole lot of other big salaries and car allowances to fund.

Restaurants and bars in downtown Louisville count on business before and after games at the Yum Center. Hotels fill up on football weekends—and they get thousands of room nights from the teams and their families who come to Louisville for the conference and NCAA tournaments that take place at the venues on Floyd Street. And not least, there's the competition from other big-time programs. Louisville did not ascend into the Atlantic Coast Conference in order to be a doormat. There's no time to rethink any of it. The machine needs to keep on running.

After Jurich was dismissed, Vince Tyra, a Louisville financier and son of a legendary U. of L. basketball player, was named interim athletic director; six months later, he was given the job on a permanent basis. Following the 2018 basketball season, he had a decision to make about the young interim coach who had stepped in for Pitino—David Padgett, who by all accounts had done an admirable job under extremely difficult circumstances.

Padgett, thirty-two years old, had served the kind of extensive apprenticeship that Jordan Fair, who came right from high school to his job at Louisville, did not. Padgett played for Pitino and then, after competing professionally in Europe for a year, came back to campus as the team's assistant strength coach. He left to serve as an assistant coach at Indiana University–Purdue University Indianapolis (known as IUPUI) for three years, and then returned as Pitino's assistant video coordinator, and later his director of operations, before finally being promoted to an assistant coaching position.

When the scandal hit and Pitino was fired, along with Fair and fellow assistant Kenny Johnson, Padgett was the last man standing. Whatever had occurred, it had not touched him. He was clean. He took over just as practice was set to begin, settled his shaken players, and led them to a 22–14 record, though they did not make the field of the NCAA tournament. Opposing coaches, his own players, and the university administration praised the poise and the class that he showed. But there was never really a chance that he was going to be kept on.

"We all owe a debt of gratitude to David," Tyra said in announcing that Padgett was done. In explaining why he was making a change, Tyra said, "We need an elite coach."

And that, of course, had everything to do with money and virtually nothing to do with Padgett's integrity, his qualities as a role model, or even his coaching ability. When I talked with Tyra, he said his first task after taking over for Jurich had been to "quarantine" the basketball program and make sure its problem did not infect the whole athletic department. Padgett had taken care of that for him. His players stayed clear of any scandal. Thrown into a difficult situation, and put under a public spotlight, they competed honorably and never complained. By all appearances, they were model student-athletes.

But just as Jurich hired Pitino to excite the fan base, Tyra recruited and landed Chris Mack, an accomplished coach at Xavier in Cincinnati, to bring some buzz back to the Yum Center. Mack's team had been awarded a No. 1 seed in the 2018 NCAA tournament, a significant achievement for a team outside one of the Power Five conferences, though they were upset in the second round. He was what's known as a "hot coach." Lots of schools wanted to hire him.

When I reminded Tyra of why Jurich went after Pitino so aggressively—to build excitement and generate revenue—he said, "I had the same sentiments as Tom on that front."

Mack will earn $4 million a year at Louisville, but because he was still under contract at his former job, the U. of L. also had to pay for his $2.9 million buyout at Xavier. Mack would be taxed on that, so Louisville also agreed to make a "gross-up" payment to him to cover it—raising the cost of extracting their new coach from his previous commitment to an estimated $4.5 million.

Incredibly, it revealed that the money would be taken from liquidated endowment funds—the same practice that the forensic audit criticized.

A t the heart of the NCAA is not just hypocrisy, but a central mythology. As fans, we want and perhaps need to believe we are watching something more admirable than pro sport: athletes who are playing for some pure love of the game and for their schools.

Otherwise, what's the allure of March Madness? It's not the best basketball in the world. College players, even the best of them, commit more senseless turnovers than NBA players do. They miss more foul shots and brick more open jumpers. Major college basketball is akin to Triple A baseball but with more pageantry and better marketing—or the NBA's G League, its developmental circuit, which draws modest crowds in cities like Canton, Ohio; Sioux Falls, Iowa; and Reno, Nevada.

NCAA players and their parents invest in the mythology—or at the very least, in the fiction of amateur basketball. They play along, to an extent, while taking a hard-eyed view of the marketplace. They see that their sons have market value. If money is offered, they take it. Not every family, but lots of them.

But with grassroots basketball now a focus of law enforcement, young players and their families have been interviewed by the FBI. They've sat in interrogation rooms, surrounded by agents. None have been charged, but they have felt the threat.

Nothing is more likely to break the bond between African American families and the NCAA than law officers rummaging around in grassroots basketball and criminalizing what were previously, at most, NCAA violations. Parents of African American sons already feel plenty of fear that their boys may suffer from heavy-handed police enforcement.

"The most significant thing is that the dialogue has been opened up," David Robinson said after the NCAA commission released its report. But the arrests and the pure filth and hypocrisy exposed by the FBI seem to call for more urgent solutions than an ongoing dialogue. And there are more potent and prominent voices speaking out about overturning some of the NCAA's central assumptions.

At MIT's Sloan Sports Athletics Conference in 2018, former president Barack Obama, a lifelong and knowledgeable basketball fan, called on the NBA to "create a well-structured" developmental league, "so that the NCAA is not serving as a farm system for the NBA, with a bunch of kids who are unpaid but are under enormous financial pressure." LeBron James is not only the NBA's best player, but its most influential. After the federal charges were announced, he blasted the NCAA as "corrupt" and strongly hinted that he would not be in favor of his son, LeBron Jr., who is thirteen years old and one of the top-rated players in his age group, playing college basketball.

It is not a good omen for the NCAA to have turned Obama and LeBron against it, and their voices may have already emboldened others. After the end of the 2018 season, Wendell Carter, a six-foot-ten forward, was one of four Duke freshmen to renounce his remaining three years of NCAA eligibility and enter the NBA draft. His mother, Kylia Carter, said that while he had enjoyed his one season at Duke, the NCAA system was indefensible. Speaking to the Knight Commission on Intercollegiate Athletics, she said, "When you remove all the bling and the bells and the sneakers and all that, you've paid for a child to come to your school to do what you wanted them to do for you, for free, and you made a lot of money when he did that, and you've got all these rules in place that say he cannot share in any of that. The only other time when labor does not get paid but yet someone else gets profits and the labor is black and the profit is white, is in slavery."

Right after the conclusion of the NCAA tournament, as her son was still weighing whether to turn pro, she said, "If you look at the pros and the cons, college basketball is a big con."

It is hard to argue otherwise while the entire enterprise, dedicated to the gospel of amateurism, serves to enrich adults within it. The Justice Department may believe that college basketball needs to be cleaned up, and that their case sends that message. But the sport, as it currently exists, cannot be cleansed just by sweeping up around the corners. It has to be transformed into something that preserves the glory of the competition but does not exploit the players.

In past college basketball scandals, it has almost always been the young players who suffer the harshest consequences. In a sense, that would have to be the case. They had careers in front of them, while the hustlers who tempted them into trouble are in most cases small-time mooks with little to lose. "If taking $700 was wrong, then I was guilty," Ralph Beard, a Kentucky player in the late 1940s, told the *New York Times* in 2005, two years before his death.

Beard was a member of the U.S. team in the 1948 Olympics, and played two years in the NBA before he was banned for life. He acknowledged taking money from gambling interests, but told George Vecsey of the *Times,* "I was totally innocent of influencing games. I never had two dimes to rub together. My mother cleaned six apartments so we could have one to live in. I took the money, and that was it."

Connie Hawkins grew up in the Bedford-Stuyvesant neighborhood of Brooklyn in the 1940s and 1950s and achieved the status of New York playground legend while he was still in his mid-teens. Larry Brown, a Hall of Fame coach and contemporary of Hawkins in Brooklyn, said of him, "He was Julius before Julius. He was Elgin before Elgin. He was Michael before Michael," referring to Julius Erving, Elgin Baylor, and Michael Jordan. "He was simply the greatest individual player I have ever seen."

Hawkins was never indicted or even directly implicated, but it was said that he introduced other players to a game fixer—an allegation he denied, and that evidence which came out later indicated was probably not true. Nevertheless, the University of Iowa, where he was a freshman and had yet to even play a game, sent him home, and he spent the first part of his professional career playing for the Globetrotters and in the old American Basketball Association.

Hawkins had plenty of talent left when he was let into the NBA at age twenty-seven, enough to score 44 points and grab 20 rebounds in a game during his rookie season with the Phoenix Suns. He averaged more than 20 points a game in his first three years in the NBA, but then quickly trailed off, even though he would hang on for another four seasons.

He was elected to basketball's Hall of Fame in 1992, which was more an acknowledgment of the injustice done to him than of the body of his work. The first half of his career was stolen from him.

Brian Bowen Jr.'s lawyer, Jason Setchen, traveled to Louisville periodically to talk to officials in the athletic department and try, unsuccessfully, to get them to let Bowen play or at least to practice with the team, and also to lend some emotional support to his client. One evening, Tugs sat in Setchen's hotel room and talked about his first-semester college experience. He was trying to keep as low a profile as possible and just go to class and get good grades, so he could move on to some other school if that became necessary.

He thought people sometimes looked at him like he was the one who brought Pitino down, which he found uncomfortable. He was easily recognizable with his six-foot-seven frame and Odell Beckham–style strip of bleached-blond hair, which Setchen suggested he consider changing up. "He has that crazy hair," Setchen said. "I've tried to say something like, 'You'd be a little less conspicuous with a more normal haircut,' but it's no use." Having lost so much else, he wasn't willing to give up his trademark look.

That night, Tugs talked about his relationship with Christian Dawkins. He said he had leaned on him to help navigate the thicket of recruiting because Dawkins seemed like a reliable, plugged-in guy from back home in Saginaw. He was a safe harbor, someone he could ask, "'Is this a trustworthy guy?' Anytime I need to ask anything, whether it's just about a coach or about the team, just anything at all, that's a guy I could go to." If the government allegations are true, he said, "I'm really mad, you know, at him. For putting me in this position."

Bowen was allowed to go to Louisville basketball games, but he stayed away. He did not want to be a spectacle—the kid who ended Pitino's reign—or a distraction to the players he still considered his teammates. The TV cameras would surely find him if he showed up at the Yum Center, and all the bloggers on the basketball sites would have a field day. His picture would end up on the front page of the *Courier-Journal* sports section.

He was living in Billy Minardi Hall, the dorm named for Pitino's late brother-in-law (and the site of the stripper parties). "I stay back in my room and watch the games on TV," he said. "My teammates have been supportive. They're cool with me. I've got to stay strong for my parents. Everybody has my back. My supporting cast is great."

He had walked over to the hotel with his parents, who were still living in Louisville. They were waiting downstairs for him. On the subject of his father, Tugs was muted. He seemed shocked, sad, and riven by a mix of complicated emotions he could not yet come to terms with. It's not like anyone could have warned him that his father was someone to avoid on the recruiting trail. He was his dad's project, and the whole thing had worked beautifully, all the way up to the point when he was about to emerge into major college basketball, just one step from the ultimate destination of the NBA.

Tugs had cared so much about becoming a player with a national reputation. Now he had one, but it was soiled. Even if he made it to the NBA, he would forever be known as the player at the center of a scandal.

He did not want to think that his father took money, and said he would not directly address it with him. "I don't want to know anything about it," he said. "I just want to see what happens with all the outcomes and everything. I've let him know, you know, I'm very upset as far as not being able to play and everything, but as far as, you know, the investigation and all that. I just brush past that."

Just before Thanksgiving, Louisville announced that Bowen would never be allowed to play for them. They were cutting ties and moving on. "Brian has been a responsible young man for the institution since he enrolled," Vince Tyra, the athletic director, said. "He has endeared himself to his teammates and the men's basketball staff with a positive attitude during a very difficult period."

In December 2017, having completed his fall semester at Louisville, Bowen transferred to the University of South Carolina, which awarded him a basketball scholarship—an indication that administrators there believed his account that he was not personally involved in any payoffs. Unlike at Louisville, he was allowed to practice with the team. "I can tell you, after being around him for three months, he's an unbelievable kid," his coach at South Carolina, Frank Martin, said.

There has been no indication that Brian Bowen Jr. is telling anything but the truth. He would not be the first high school prospect whose services were exchanged for money, but who did not personally see any of it. In fact, there are plenty of people familiar with recruiting's dark side who would say that this is the norm, not the exception. Even if he *did* know what was going on behind the scenes, or had some notion of it, he was not controlling the situation. His father and Christian Dawkins were running his recruiting. There was no guarantee Tugs would ever play for South Carolina. The NCAA would have to rule that he was eligible. One holdup was that they wanted him to account for the money that came from Dawkins. How was that impermissible benefit spent? He kept telling them he had no idea because he didn't know anything about it in the first place.

Tugs declared provisionally for the NBA draft, just in case he was not ruled eligible to play for South Carolina. But his greatest hope was to play NCAA basketball. He was a believer. "I want to eventually play in the NBA, but I love college basketball," he said. "You know, the tournament, March Madness, all that stuff. That's been like my dream since I was really little, to experience it at least just once."

In May 2018, the NCAA let him know that he would not be allowed to play in the coming season. "I am completely devastated," he said.

ACKNOWLEDGMENTS

This book is drawn in part from my interviews with several of the people who figure prominently in it, including Rick Pitino, Tom Jurich, and Brian Bowen Jr.

Jurich, the former athletic director at the University of Louisville, was generous with his time in talking to me about his two decades on the job, and he and his wife, Terrilynn, also made sure I saw some of Steamboat Springs, Colorado, where they retreated after leaving Louisville.

Jason Setchen, Brian Bowen Jr.'s lawyer, has represented numerous college athletes and was invaluable in providing insights into how the NCAA deals with young players who become the subjects of its investigations.

Among the people who helped me understand the university and the culturally and socially complex city that surrounds it were Louisville's longtime mayor, Jerry Abramson, and Keith Runyon, Terry Meiners, Emily Bingham, Craig Greenberg, Karen Williams,

ACKNOWLEDGMENTS

Jonathan Blue, Tim Sullivan, Chris Otts, and Jere Downs. Ian Shapira, a Louisville native and ardent U. of L. basketball fan, helped interpret his hometown and offered valuable suggestions.

At the University of Louisville, Kenny Klein, the longtime sports information director, was unfailingly helpful and professional in responding to my many requests. Vince Tyra, the new athletic director, made time for an interview even as he continued to remake the athletic department after the departures of Pitino and Jurich.

Louisville is small enough that its civic leaders overlap on various boards and may be allies in one realm and adversaries in another—and it is Southern enough that its people do not like to offend. There were several Louisvillians who aided in my understanding of the city and its personalities who asked that their names not appear in these pages. I am grateful for their contributions.

I owe thanks to Herb Sendek, the head basketball coach at Santa Clara and a former Pitino assistant; and to Sonny Vaccaro, Tom Konchalski, and Adam Zagoria for their wisdom about the worlds of grassroots basketball and college recruiting. There were, as well, numerous people within the basketball fraternity who spoke to me on the condition that I not include their names.

Jonathan Jensen, a sports marketing professor at the University of North Carolina, educated me on the thicket of relationships between the NCAA, its member institutions, the shoe companies, and various other commercial entities.

As I write this, the innocence or guilt of the defendants in the criminal case involving college basketball has yet to be determined, and there are serious questions about the legal theories used by the government in bringing their charges. But the broader truths that the FBI and federal prosecutors have revealed—of shady practices on the recruiting trail and exploitation of young athletes—are indisputable. Hundreds of pages of court documents have been filed in the case, and the story they tell has informed my reporting and writing.

From the time the charges were announced on September 26, 2017, the case has been exhaustively covered by journalists working across the spectrum of print, broadcast, and online media, and my research has benefitted from their excellent work. I want to mention several who have led the ongoing coverage and whose work I have found particularly helpful: Pat Forde and Pete Thamel of Yahoo! News; Mark Schlabach, Jeff Goodman, Steve Fainaru, and Mark Fainaru-Wada of ESPN; Will Hobson of the *Washington Post*; Ben Cohen of the *Wall Street Journal*; and Marc Tracy of the *New York Times*.

In Louisville, the *Courier-Journal* has covered the U. of L. angle aggressively, and the investigative team at the television station WDRB has done several years of impressive reporting on the university's tangled finances. Both are a reminder that vigorous local reporting remains essential.

I have benefited, as well, from the professional and personal support that every author needs to successfully and sanely reach the finish line. My editor, Scott Moyers, urged me to set off on this project and guided me through it with his usual deft touch and good cheer. His assistant, Mia Council, helped keep me on course. Andrew Wylie and Jacqueline Ko at the Wylie Agency were there, as always, to serve as my allies, sounding boards, and advocates.

My wife, Ann Gerhart, has been my closest partner in every way for more than three decades, including journalistically, and she has listened and advised me through the course of this book even as she does her own work as a senior editor at the *Washington Post*, where it's been a bit busy lately.

ACKNOWLEDGMENTS

My daughter Sofia Sokolove, in her off hours from her own demanding writing and editing position, contributed many hours of research and was the incisive first reader of the manuscript. I now have the enormous good fortune to have another crack journalist with a finely tuned ear to check my thinking and punch up my writing. (Or, as Ann and I like to say, Sofia has joined the family business—if it actually is one.)

INDEX

INDEX